Linger in My Presence

ISBN 978-1-952320-13-2 (Paperback)
Linger in My Presence
Copyright © 2020 Debbie Furey
All rights reserved.

No part of this publication may be reproduced, distributed, or transmitted in any form or by any means, including photocopying, recording, or other electronic or mechanical methods, without the prior written permission of the publisher, except in the case of brief quotations embodied in critical reviews and certain other noncommercial uses permitted by copyright law.

For permission requests, write to the publisher at the address below.

Yorkshire Publishing
4613 E. 91st St,
Tulsa, OK 74137
www.YorkshirePublishing.com
918.394.2665

Printed in the USA

Linger in My Presence

A Devotional in Poetry of
Conversations with God

DEBBIE FUREY

TULSA

I dedicate this book to my dear friends, Margie Mihalic, Karen Hertzig my sister, Sandy Skillen, and Gloria Baldauff who have prayed with me and for me. They are women who linger in God's Presence and shine with His glory. I thank God for their friendship and love. I especially want to thank Sandy Skillen and Karen Hertzig for their help in editing this book and the time they put into it.

Table of Contents

Invitation to Linger in My Presence ix
Introduction xi

Chapter 1 – It's All About the Blood 1
Chapter 2 – Reflections of His Glory 24
Chapter 3 – Come Up Higher 50
Chapter 4 – God is Light 72
Chapter 5 – Bread of Life 97
Chapter 6 – Great Grace 116
Chapter 7 – Go Beyond the Veil 134
Chapter 8 – Linger in My Presence 161

Invitation to Linger in My Presence

Linger—stay in a place longer than necessary because of a reluctance to leave.

When I asked the Lord what the title of this book should be, "Linger in My Presence," came into my mind. Then I wrote down what I thought I heard Him say:

Come and linger in My Presence. I have much to say to you. It is only in quietness and rest you will hear My still small voice. I am always near, and even though I know your thoughts, I long to hear you talk to Me about all that concerns your everyday life.

You hear My voice more than you realize—as I speak to you through others, through your thoughts, the beauty of creation, or even in unusual circumstances that you can't explain away.

My voice and My ways are hidden from the rebellious and proud lest they should see with their eyes and hear with their ears. Isaiah 6:9-10.

Come, draw near in faith with love for Me in your heart, that springs from the hope you have in Me. Colossians 1:3-6. I am the lover of your soul and will perfect all that concerns you.

Come, I invite you to linger in My Presence…A way has been made through the cross…The veil separating the Holy Place from the Holy of Holies has come down…Come Linger in My Presence.

Introduction

God often speaks to us in earthly pictures or symbols using things that we are familiar with to help us realize His eternal truths. One of the amazing Old Testament pictures is the Courtyard and Temple. Filled with earthly items such as an altar, basin (sea), steps, doorway, lampstands, bread, curtain and a priest with earthly things to do, God reveals the way to His Presence that the priest would have to follow for the people of God to be forgiven and in relationship with Him. For us, a spiritual journey with prophetic pictures is revealed and is still very real today.

In 1 Peter 2:9, believers are called a royal priesthood, a holy nation. When Jesus died on the cross, the Temple curtain or veil, leading into the Holy of Holies was split in two, symbolizing access for God's people into the Presence of God. The priests began the journey to the Holy of Holies at the altar located in the courtyard of the Temple. The sacrifices offered on the altar were a prophetic picture of the Lamb of God (Jesus) dying for our sins. The priest had to start here to be able to proceed into the Temple.

By faith, believers can proceed toward the Temple, like the ancient priests. The item next encountered was called the

Sea or Basin. Here, the priests would have cleansed themselves after offering the sacrifices before proceeding into the Temple. This is symbolic or prophetic of believers washing themselves with the water of the Word of God—reading the Bible and putting it into practice.

Next are steps leading up into the Temple and a door—a Way of Entrance. This is a picture of believers ascending toward our secret place where we meet with God daily to pray and worship and Jesus being our Way.

As you go through the Temple doors by faith, the room before you was called the Holy Place. In this room were three items. The first item was the Lampstand or Menorah. The second item was the table for the Bread of the Presence. The third item in the Holy Place was the Golden Altar of Incense before which the priests offered up daily incense to God. We will see the prophetic application of these items in the coming chapters.

Behind the Holy Place, and separated from it by a heavy curtain, was the Holy of Holies. It was a room with no windows, and within its walls was the Ark of the Covenant. The lid of the Ark represented the Mercy Seat of God. The Manifest Presence, or Shekinah Glory of God, dwelt there continually and was the light. To not pass through the curtain would be to fall short of God's glory, fellowship, communion and to continue to be separated from Him. Jesus' death and sacrifice tore the curtain, giving us access to the Presence of God. We can be forever changed from glory to glory as we are transformed by His Presence dwelling in us.

The poems I have written are placed into chapters and depict our journey into the Holy of Holies, where we can linger in His Presence.

A part of praying is not only speaking, but also listening for what God might be telling us. As I composed these poems, I wrote what I was saying to God, but also what I felt He was saying to me. I have always sensed their message was to be shared with the church, the bride of Christ. Reading my poems often draws me closer to the Lord. My hope and prayer is that you will experience the Lord speaking to you as you enjoy reading them.

CHAPTER 1

It's All About the Blood

The Altar—It's All About the Blood

Coming into the Temple compound, the first thing you would see would be the altar where they sacrificed animals to the Lord. Ever since the fall of Adam and Eve, shed blood has been required for the forgiveness of sins. Adam and Eve used fig leaves to cover their nakedness, but the Lord replaced those garments with garments made of animal skin. An animal had to be slain for that. Both Cain and Abel knew a blood sacrifice was required in Genesis 4:1-7. That was the pattern in the Bible until Christ was offered as the last sacrifice for the sins of the world. The following poems are about Jesus making a way to Heaven for us through His death on the cross. For you see...It's All About the Blood.

It's All About the Blood

It's all about the blood, my Savior shed for me
The perfect sacrifice was offered and nailed upon a tree
From the foundation of the earth, a plan was put in place
Repentance is the key to accessing God's redeeming grace

"It's all about the blood," the Lord explained to Cain
Rejecting God's advice led to his brother being slain
Sin desires to have you, it crouches at the door
Repentance is the key to bloods power to restore

John preached in Judea's desert calling people to repent
This opened hearts to Jesus' message everywhere He went
Prepare the way, prepare the way, it's all about the blood
Cascading from the cross of Jesus in a redeeming flood

Even in eternity, His blood will never lose its power
Humble, grateful hearts will continue to grow and flower
Walking with God, on the new earth, brought there by His grace
Because of His blood, shed for me, I'll see Him face to face

February 27, 2019

1 Peter 1:18-21 (NKJV)—"…knowing that you were not redeemed with corruptible things, like silver or gold, from your aimless conduct received by tradition from your fathers, [19] but with the precious blood of Christ, as of a lamb without blemish and without spot. [20] He indeed was foreordained before the foundation of the world, but was manifest in these last times for you [21] who through Him believe in

God, who raised Him from the dead and gave Him glory, so that your faith and hope are in God."

1 Peter 1:3-25
Genesis 4:1-12
Matthew 3:1-12
Revelation 22:1-6

Worldly Ways

Each man is born with worldly ways; it's the only reality they know
When you believe and are born again, there is a different path you must go
Make a decision to leave worldly ways and keep from acting like "mere men"
By following Christ, a new way appears, that leads to the gates of heaven

This second birth transforms "mere men," into the sons of God
We grow from servants, then friends into sons, as we travel along earth's sod
He gave the right to become children of God, to those who believe in His Name
Let us choose to be holy like our dear Father, to the world His glory proclaim

Destruction awaits those who follow the way of the world, and its passions therein
The law of the Spirit of life set me free from the deceiving power of sin
Our present sufferings cannot be compared to the glory that will be revealed
So, set your mind on what the Spirit desires, and to His ways earnestly yield

January 20, 2019

John 15:15—"I no longer call you servants, because a servant does not know his master's business. Instead, I have called you friends, for everything that I learned from my Father I have made known to you."

John 1:12-13—"Yet to all who did receive him, to those who believed in his name, he gave the right to become children of God—¹³children born not of natural descent, nor of human decision or a husband's will, but born of God."

1 Corinthians 3:1-4
Hebrews 2:10-15
Romans 8:1-27

Justified

Just as if I'd never sinned—that is how God sees me
From the law of sin and death, the Spirit set me free
For those who have the Spirit of Christ—there is no condemnation
The sons of God will be revealed in eager expectation

Crucify the sinful nature, die to its desires
The mind controlled by evil thoughts, leads to death's hot fires
Sin condemned in sinful man, by His blood soaked cross
All who choose to follow Jesus, do not suffer loss

Justified by God's own Son, we now are heirs with Him
If we share His sufferings, we'll in His glory swim
Rivers of His Holy Spirit, will flow from deep within
Testifying to a perishing world, that is lost in Adam's sin

Just as if I'd never sinned—how awesome is the thought
Our Savior paid a terrible price for salvation to be bought
Forever we'll be praising Him, on the streets of glory
"Justified by grace I am," will be the redeemed stories

January 10, 2019

Romans 8:29-30—" For those God foreknew he also predestined to be conformed to the image of his Son, that he might be the firstborn among many brothers and sisters.[30] And those he predestined, he also called; those he called, he also justified; those he justified, he also glorified."

Romans 8:1-27
John 7:37-39
Revelation 5:1-14

Follow the Call

Do not be ashamed to testify about Me
My blood was shed to purchase and redeem thee
Join with Me in suffering for the gospel's sake
The Spirit of love and power invites you to partake

Fear has no place where faith does abide
The journey is long, but I'll be your guide
Do not look back or you may stumble and fall
Put your hand to the plow and follow the call

Every need that you have I shall supply
With miraculous power I will reply
I am coming soon and My reward is with Me
To share with those who follow closely

January 23, 2018

Luke 9:61-62—"Still another said, "I will follow you, Lord; but first let me go back and say goodbye to my family." **62** Jesus replied, "No one who puts a hand to the plow and looks back is fit for service in the kingdom of God."

2 Timothy 1:7-8—"For the Spirit God gave us does not make us timid, but gives us power, love and self-discipline. **8** So do not be ashamed of the testimony about our Lord or of me his prisoner. Rather, join with me in suffering for the gospel, by the power of God."

2 Timothy 1:5-14
Hebrews 11
Revelation 22:12-17

Cup of Tears

He took a teardrop from His eye and placed it in a cup
The Lord held the chalice out to me inviting me to sup
Many tears were gathered there, filling it to the brim
"Come share with Me My sufferings," was what I heard from Him

The drink was bitter to the taste—many tears sprang from my eyes
To my ears came many sounds—sobbing's, moans and sighs
Broken hearts and shattered lives were scattered in a heap
As I looked into My Savior's eyes, we both began to weep

The walls around my heart, that once stood firm and tall
Started now to crumble, then began to fall
Whatever gains I thought I had, I now consider loss
Because I know He died for me, my boast is now the cross

I want to know His power and, in His sufferings, share
Becoming like Him in His death has set me free to care
Forgetting what is now behind, I press on toward the goal
An eternal prize is now in sight, at stake are many souls

"Come join with Me in suffering," is the battle cry
"If you lose your life for My sake, you will never die"
In death our lowly bodies we will gladly then forsake
His power will transform us, when with His likeness we awake

May 27, 2018

Philippians 3:10-11—"I want to know Christ—yes, to know the power of his resurrection and participation in his sufferings, becoming like him in his death, [11] and so, somehow, attaining to the resurrection from the dead."

Philippians 1:29—"For it has been granted to you on behalf of Christ not only to believe in him, but also to suffer for him."

Philippians 3:7-21   Matthew 10:38-39

    A story came to my mind this morning from a book* Rick Joyner wrote called, "The Final Quest." In a vision the Lord gave him, Rick saw tears in the Lord's eyes. The Lord was sharing with him His love for the lost. The Lord took a tear from His eye and placed it in a cup and offered it to Rick. As Rick drank it, he remarked he had never tasted anything so bitter. It caused a river of tears to flow from his eyes, not only for the lost, but also for the Lord. Then God's peace began to fill him with a river of love.

    As I was thinking about this, I felt like the Lord was asking me, "Would you also drink this cup with Me?" I knew I could not say no. Then the words to this poem started to appear in my thoughts. I really didn't see with my eyes or hear with my ears the Lord asking me to drink the cup of tears but I knew He was offering it to me and I wanted to be obedient. This poem touched me deeply and changed my heart. I want to have His heart for the lost because I know from His Word that if I share in His sufferings I will also share in the resurrection. Suffering for Christ always has an eternal purpose that we might never know about until we get to heaven.

    I like to read this poem often to remember His request.

* "The Final Quest," by Rick Joyner. Copywrite 1996. Used by permission www.morningstarministries.org

A Seed

Take My hand, come die with Me
For death to self, is true liberty
To bring forth life a seed must first die
Death's the only way it can multiply

A seed in its shell is protected and safe
But there is no growth in which to partake
It can't live forever in its seed like state
To fulfill its destiny, it must regenerate

A seed that is sown in the rich dark earth
Must first die to experience rebirth
The water of the Word will cause it to swell
While new life emerging will burst the hard shell

The life that comes forth is nothing like the seed
Resurrection has changed it to something new indeed!
The Lord will come to harvest His crops in the field
While new seed from its fruit will multiply its yield

The Lord of the harvest comes with sickle in hand
When the harvest is ripe throughout all the land
Both the bad and the good will be harvested then
The Tree of Life will return to the earth once again

December 22, 2017

Romans 6:3-4—"Or don't you know that all of us who were baptized into Christ Jesus were baptized into his death? [4] We were therefore buried with him through baptism into death in order that, just as Christ was raised from the dead through the glory of the Father, we too may live a new life."

Romans 6:1-14
1 Corinthians 15:35-58
Revelation 14:14-20
John 4:34-38
Revelation 21:1-3
Revelation 22:1-5

Consider It Joy

Help me to look at this differently, Lord
When persecution comes by disdainful looks or a word
If they treated You this way, why should I expect
To be treated any differently, with honor or respect?

"Don't be surprised if the world hates you
They hated Me first and My motives misconstrued
My love for them does not waver or falter
Some will relent and repent at My altar"

"Show them My love that is holy and pure
Stay close to Me, I'll help you endure
Forgiving and giving keeps your heart in tune with Me
Releasing heaven's melody deep within thee"

"Consider it joy when you encounter these trials
They are really rejecting Me by their repeated denials
Rejoice and be glad, for your reward is great
The only way to heaven is through Me—the gate"

December 12, 2017

James 1:2-3—"Consider it all joy, my brethren, when you encounter various trials,³ knowing that the testing of your faith produces endurance."

John 15:18-21
1 John 3:13
John 10:1-9

A Slave Girl Set Free

A royal blue garment in the city of David
A robe of a King that was heavily braided
The swishing of hems as feet hurry along
A crowd starts to gather into an unruly throng

A slave girl is thrown to the ground in a heap
Stifles a scream, but tears fall as she weeps
A hand is extended to her from on high
Her ransom is paid, by One crucified

Who is this King in disguise unbeknown?
Why would He depart from His heavenly throne?
To rescue those in bondage to the slavery of sin
Granting a pardon and peace deep within

It is Jesus who walks along earth's darkest streets
His victory has purchased His enemies defeat
A ransom was paid for all those hell bound
To those who accept Him as Savior and King crowned

This slave girl was rescued and set free to live
Dressed in a white robe, told to love and forgive
Now she walks along with her Savior and King
To help rescue others and His praises to sing

January 6, 2018

Isaiah 49:8-9—"This is what the Lord says: "In the time of my favor I will answer you, and in the day of salvation I will help you; I will keep you and will make you to be a covenant for the people, to restore the land and to reassign its desolate inheritances, ⁹ to say to the captives, 'Come out,' and to those in darkness, 'Be free!'"

Hosea 2
Isaiah 49
Isaiah 61

He Was Assigned a Grave

He was assigned a grave with the wicked in death
When the enemy came calling to steal away His breath
A pauper's field was all the crucified could afford
An undignified death was the sinner's reward

Like a lamb to the slaughter our Savior was led
For the sins of many His blood was shed
It was the Father's will that He suffered death's pain
A guilt offering was paid so we have heaven to gain

We all, like sheep, have gone astray
Each of us has turned to his own way
The Father, on Jesus, laid the iniquity of us all
Regaining Eden's garden lost in Adam's fall

He was assigned a grave with the rich in His death
A tomb fit for a King in the solid rock was cleft
A way was opened up to the throne room on high
By a sacrifice of His blood were many justified

By oppression and judgment Jesus was taken away
But arose from the dead after ransom was paid
When He ascended on high, He led captives in His train
Now all who believe have mercy and heaven to gain

October 20, 2017

Isaiah 53:9—"He was assigned a grave with the wicked, and with the rich in his death, though he had done no violence, nor was any deceit in his mouth."

Leviticus 5:14-19
Isaiah 53
Matthew 27:57-60
Luke 23:50-53
Psalm 68:18-20
Ephesians 4:7-10

    Jesus was assigned both a grave with the wicked and with the rich. The bodies that were crucified at that time were not always claimed, and the unclaimed ones probably would have been thrown in a pit together. Since most of those crucified were criminals or political foes, there would have been shame in claiming the bodies. Luke 23 records Joseph of Arimathea going to Pilate and asking for Jesus' body. He did that because Jesus' body was assigned to go somewhere else. Because of Joseph, the assignment was changed to a rich man's tomb carved out of a rock. The prophecy of Isaiah 53:9 was fulfilled literally—Jesus was assigned both a grave with the wicked and the rich.
    We also are assigned a grave with the wicked and the rich _if_ we are a believer in Christ Jesus. Because of Adam's sin and our sin, we deserve death and our physical bodies will die. But because Christ paid our ransom, the assignment is changed to the inheritance of life forever with Christ. There, we will experience the riches of God's glory.

The First Gift at Christmas

This little babe laid in manger bare
Will return one day, with the saints in the air
Crowned as King, He will reign upon the earth
Who could have imagined this, at His humble birth?

Hidden were God's motives, under wondrous star
Wise men came with gifts, traveling from afar
Written in the heavens, was a glowing sign
The story of redemption, as the galaxies aligned

The angels declared God's glory, in the chilly night
Startling watching shepherds, drenched in holy fright
They hurried to the babe—the angel's message to impart
Causing all who heard, to ponder in their heart

The very first gift at Christmas, was a swaddled child
Those who believe in Him, with God are reconciled
Announce the angel's message— "Peace to man on earth"
Our Savior came to die—to proclaim mankind's worth

December 23, 2018

John 3:16-17—"For God so loved the world that he gave his one and only Son, that whoever believes in him shall not perish but have eternal life. [17] For God did not send his Son into the world to condemn the world, but to save the world through him."

Genesis 1:14 (KJV)—"And God said, "Let there be lights in the firmament of the heaven to divide the day from the night; and let them be for signs, and for seasons, and for days, and years."

Matthew 2:1-2—"Now when Jesus was born in Bethlehem of Judaea in the days of Herod the king, behold, there came wise men from the east to Jerusalem, ² Saying, Where is he that is born King of the Jews? for we have seen his star in the east, and are come to worship him."

Revelation 19:11-16
Luke 2:1-20
Matthew 2:1-12
Psalm 19:1-4
John 3:16-21

Vast is His Love

"How much do you love me?", the little girl asked
Her dad opened his arms wide and acted aghast
"Why, deeper than the ocean and wider than the sea
That is how much I love you and what you mean to me"

"How much do you love me?", the teenager asked
An uncomfortable silence followed, his eyes were downcast
"I can't marry you, sorry, but it won't work out
My future is uncertain, my feelings are in doubt"

We search the world over to answer that same question
The answer eludes us with only mere suggestion
Our search for significance can only then be found
In knowing God's love, so vast and profound

Jesus came to give life, but accomplished it by dying
Answering our question, while they were crucifying
"How much do you love me?" He opened His arms wide
"This much," His eyes replied, as He bowed His head and died

April 18, 2019

John 3:16-18—"For God so loved the world that he gave his one and only Son, that whoever believes in him shall not perish but have eternal life. ¹⁷ For God did not send his Son into the world to condemn the world, but to save the world through him. ¹⁸ Whoever believes in him is not condemned, but whoever does not believe stands condemned already because they have not believed in the name of God's one and only Son."

John 19

Release the Horses

Victors ride white horses, saddle up and go
Strong is the battle—mighty is the foe
Ride victoriously forward; your Captain leads the way
Galloping on warhorses, charging into battle's fray

Steam from flaring nostrils, rises in the air
Hooves like flint strike sparks, from each courageous mare
Leaping over barriers, crossing rivers wide
Victors hang on tightly—to your mighty ride

The horses fear not battle's might, pressing on ahead
Weapons clash on every side leaving many dead
The enemy may outnumber, but you don't have to fear
The Lord is on your side, and is always near

Release the horses and their riders at the Lord's command
He paid the price with His blood that the law demands
Now He comes to rescue those, caught in Satan's lies
Do not fear to join this battle, until He occupies

June 3, 2019

Psalm 45:3-5—"Gird your sword on your side, you mighty one; clothe yourself with splendor and majesty. [4] In your majesty ride forth victoriously in the cause of truth, humility and justice; let your right hand achieve awesome deeds. [5] Let your sharp arrows pierce the hearts of the king's enemies; let the nations fall beneath your feet."

Deuteronomy 20:1—"When you go to war against your enemies and see horses and chariots and an army greater than yours, do not be afraid of them, because the Lord your God, who brought you up out of Egypt, will be with you."

Job 39:19-25
Ephesians 6:10-20
Revelation 19:11-14

If you could pull back the veil separating the natural world from the spiritual world, things would look very different. Horses are symbolic of ministries, movements, and churches that we ride along with to do the Lord's will and to battle the forces of evil here on the earth to set the captives free. At the end of the age, when the Lord returns to earth with His saints, we will also be riding out of Heaven with Him on white horses for the last battle as He fights to reclaim what is His— the earth. (Revelation 19).

CHAPTER 2

Reflections of His Glory

The Sea or Bronze Basin—Reflections of His Glory

In the courtyard, between the altar and the front of the Temple, stood a huge reservoir of water called the sea. It was made of bronze and was used by the priests for ritual cleansing. This washing ritual was to prepare the priests to enter the Holy Place at the top of the steps leading into the Temple. It represented washing away all the worldly ways and sins that clung to them. Jesus is the Word of God and we are washed with water through the Word in Ephesians 5:25-27. Water satisfies our thirst, waters creation, and also fills up deep wells, which is a picture of the deep things of God. Water also reflects images and we are to reflect the nature of Jesus in all we do so I titled this chapter—Reflections of His Glory.

Reflections of His Glory

My desire is to know You and love You even more
I delight in Your Presence as I worship and adore
Come closer; fill me; with Your truth and grace
In faith I am believing we are speaking face-to-face

Wash me with Your Word, so my mind can be renewed
Cleansing deep within—changing thoughts and attitude
Until with unveiled face, Your glory I reflect
Transform me to Your likeness, which is holy and perfect

There is a poor reflection gazing back at me
In the mirror of my soul a distortion I do see
Now I know in part, but will one day fully know
Your depth of love and mercy, You do on me bestow

Your treasure is stored in me, a fragile jar of clay
It is in my brokenness, Your glory does display
That shows this all surpassing power, is from God alone
Let all the glory go to Jesus, now seated on His throne

April 6, 2019

2 Corinthians 3:18—"And we all, who with unveiled faces reflect the Lord's glory, are being transformed into his image with ever-increasing glory, which comes from the Lord, who is the Spirit."

1 Corinthians 13:12—"For now we see only a reflection as in a mirror; then we shall see face to face. Now I know in part; then I shall know fully, even as I am fully known."

Psalm 17:15
1 John 3:1-3
2 Corinthians 4

Well of Never-Ending Water

God is always speaking, but often we don't hear
We feel He stands afar off, but He is always near
Even when we turn away, He bids us, "Come, return—
There is much I want to give you, much that you must learn"

"Come aside and join Me, at our secret place
Waiting there for you, is My mercy, love and grace
My well of never-ending water, will refresh your soul
Come with hopeful heart to draw, and drink till you are full"

"Then, when you have drunk your fill, give some to your brother
The world will want to know of Me, when you have love for each other
You are in Me and I am in you—we are truly one
Because I live, you also will live, when your earthly days are done"

"If you love Me, you will obey—and follow until the end
When you do what I command, you are then My friend
There is no greater thing to do, than love each other well
Let others know about the place, where forever we will dwell"

June 19, 2019

John 4:10-14—"Jesus answered her, "If you knew the gift of God and who it is that asks you for a drink, you would have asked him and he would have given you living water."

[11] "Sir," the woman said, "You have nothing to draw with and the well is deep. Where can you get this living water? [12] Are

you greater than our father Jacob, who gave us the well and drank from it himself, as did also his sons and his livestock?"

¹³ Jesus answered, "Everyone who drinks this water will be thirsty again, ¹⁴ but whoever drinks the water I give them will never thirst. Indeed, the water I give them will become in them a spring of water welling up to eternal life."

John 15:14—"You are my friends if you do what I command."

John 4:4-42
John 14:15-21

River of Life

The river of life flows free and fast
Whoever will enter, can on Me, their fears cast
The deeper you go, the more you'll be set free
Drink deep of My Word, then with My eyes, you will see

This river slows to a trickle for the selfish and the proud
Thoughts of gain is their goal from earth's clamoring crowd
They have distanced themselves by their sin and their pride
Return, oh return; draw close and abide

I will extend peace like a river till it forms a flooding stream
My Spirit will I pour out, in visions and in dreams
On your sons and your daughters, to those humble and pure
I will show wonders in heaven to help them endure

This river of life cascades from My throne
Watering trees with healing leaves, producing fruit now unknown
Come, if you are thirsty, it is free to all
To those who seek My mercy and on My name call

March 28, 2019

John 7:37-38—"On the last and greatest day of the festival, Jesus stood and said in a loud voice, "Let anyone who is thirsty come to me and drink. **38** Whoever believes in me, as Scripture has said, rivers of living water will flow from within them."

Psalm 46:4—"There is a river whose streams make glad the city of God, the holy place where the Most High dwells."

Revelation 22:1-2—"Then the angel showed me the river of the water of life, as clear as crystal, flowing from the throne of God and of the Lamb ² down the middle of the great street of the city. On each side of the river stood the tree of life, bearing twelve crops of fruit, yielding its fruit every month. And the leaves of the tree are for the healing of the nations."

Isaiah 66:12-14
Ezekiel 47:1-12
John 4:10-14

Worthless Idols

We make them in our heart, fashioned in our mind
Idols of our choosing, idols of our kind
What are those things we trust in—cherish above all?
Is it people, things or money our foolish hearts enthrall?

We think these idols save us, give us life and joy
But they are meant to charm us, distract and then destroy
We make them with our hands, and then hold them in our heart
Causing passion for our God and King slowly to depart

My people have forsaken Me, a spring of living water
I've redeemed you from a slave—to My son and daughter
When you forsake the Lord your God and have no awe of Me
Your wickedness will punish you throughout eternity

Return to Me, declares the Lord, for I am merciful
Acknowledge the rebellion of your faithless soul
Then I will give you shepherds, after My own heart
They'll lead back to living waters, never to depart

January 13, 2018

Jeremiah 2:5—"This is what the LORD says: "What fault did your ancestors find in me, that they strayed so far from me? They followed worthless idols and became worthless themselves."

Romans 11:22 (NASB)—" Behold then the kindness and severity of God; to those who fell, severity, but to you,

God's kindness, if you continue in His kindness; otherwise you also will be cut off."

Jeremiah 2
Jeremiah 3
Revelation 3:15-16
Hebrews 10:26-39
Romans 11:17-23
2 Peter 2:20-22
John 15:5-6

    The past few nights, I've awakened after 2:00 AM and couldn't go back to sleep. Then, again, last night, the clock read 2:05 as I awoke from a deep sleep. A thought came to my mind that it was a Bible verse, so I arose and opened the book and it went to Jeremiah. I then turned to Jeremiah 2:5. This poem came to me after I read the next few chapters.
    * The following is an excerpt from Rick Joyner's email on "The Kindness and Severity of God":

    <u>Some of the most destructive false doctrines and heresies have come from those who could not</u> **"behold now the kindness and the severity of God" (see Romans 11:22).** <u>If we cannot see both of these, then we do not know God, as He is and are worshipping a God we have made, which is an idol.</u> He is more kind and gracious than any human will ever be, but He is also severe. Drawing His wrath should be the greatest fear of every human being.
    As we are told in Romans 2:4, it is **"the kindness of God"** that leads us repentance. Who can truly see His kindness and grace and not worship Him? We will be worshiping and thanking Him forever for His mercy and grace. The fear of His wrath may not draw men to Him, but it has certainly

driven many to Him. The first Great Awakening was ignited by a sermon by Jonathan Edwards entitled, "Sinners in the Hands of an Angry God." Many other great revivals were sparked by preaching on the severity of God. It may be better to be drawn than driven, but it is better to be driven than to not come at all.

That being understood, those drawn to Him because of His kindness often tend to think that His kindness is all there is to know about Him. If we do not mature beyond that in our knowledge of Him, we will be prone to embrace "hyper-grace" deceptions. These are in need of studying His judgments and His wrath, which are abundant in both the Old and New Testaments.

Likewise, those who have been driven to the Lord by fear of His severity can also be deceived about Him, thinking that He is only a harsh curmudgeon with no humor and no tolerance for sinners. He loves sinners—all of them—and desires for them to be saved. He had much more grace for sinners than He did the self-righteous. He is full of grace and mercy, and He prefers mercy over judgment. However, He has limits, and when those limits are reached, it is a fearful thing to behold.

To see Him as He is, we must see Him as utterly kind and utterly severe at the same time. He is severe because He loves us. Love is His nature, but it is a severe love. Think about this: Jesus walked the earth as an exact representation of the Father. He called some of the roughest men that could probably be found to be His disciples. Even after living with Him for three and a half years, these tough characters were still afraid to ask Him a question on the night before He was crucified! He was obviously intimidating, but He could also be so gentle and merciful to children and to sinners.

To know God as He is, and to not distort the Scriptures, we must reconcile both God's kindness and His severity in our hearts, seeing Him as He is and not as we may want Him to be. As we mature, we will come to understand that He is perfect, and so are His judgments.

*"The Kindness and Severity of God," by Rick Joyner. Word for the Week 3, 2018. Used by permission. https://publications.morningstarministries.org/word-for-the-week/kindness-and-severity-god-book-revelation

Produce Fruit in Keeping with Repentance

The axe is already laid to the root of the trees
But the ones bearing good fruit, I'll let them be
Iniquity will not stand in My Holy Place above
Heaven is for those filled with faith, hope and love

Therefore, produce fruit in keeping with repentance
You once stood condemned under sins deadly sentence
Now you are set free by My shed blood alone
I already paid the price for your sin to atone

Now walk in My freedom without condemnation
New life in the Spirit is yours through salvation
The mind controlled by My Spirit produces peace and life
While the sinful nature brings hostility and strife

There is a choice, every day, on which path to walk
Study My Word so your ways will match your talk
Sin deceives, then defiles, finally deadening the heart
Stay close to Me, so My holiness I can impart

Christ in you is your hope and your glory
Walking in holiness is now mandatory
Only the pure in heart will see God's face
You can't do it on your own—ask for My mercy and grace

June 26, 2018

Matthew 3:10-11—"The ax is already at the root of the trees, and every tree that does not produce good fruit will be cut down and thrown into the fire.

¹¹ "I baptize you with water for repentance. But after me comes one who is more powerful than I, whose sandals I am not worthy to carry. He will baptize you with the Holy Spirit and fire."

Hebrews 12:4-6—"In your struggle against sin, you have not yet resisted to the point of shedding your blood. ⁵ And have you completely forgotten this word of encouragement that addresses you as a father addresses his son? It says, "My son, do not make light of the Lord's discipline, and do not lose heart when he rebukes you, ⁶ because the Lord disciplines the one he loves, and he chastens everyone he accepts as his son."

Matthew 3:7-12
Romans 8:1-17
James 1:12-27
Colossians 3:1-17

As I was reading about John the Baptist in Matthew 3:7-12 this morning, I came upon something I wrote in my bible that was a teaching from Francis Frangipane about producing fruit in keeping with repentance. I can't remember what book I got these from, but his words are a good example of true repentance.

- We do not cease turning from pride until we delight in lowliness
- We continue to repent of selfishness until love flows naturally from us
- We do not stop mourning our impurities until we are pure

- Repentance is not burdensome except to those who refuse correction
- As long as we desire to be like Him, His rebuke will be a door into His Presence— Revelation 3:19
- If you recoil at the word repentance, it is because you do not want to change

by Francis Frangipane

Like a Tree

What can bear the weight of a house's outer shell?
What can tell of heaven's glory or the pains of hell?
What can bridge a span of water bearing all your weight?
Or protect you with a fence, bearing swinging gate?

These are products of a tree standing straight and tall
Who can tell of all its uses, products great and small?
The tree of life in Eden's garden promised many things
The tree on which our Savior hung reversed death's evil sting

What is the fruit you will produce to be offered on that "Day"?
Did your roots hold firm to the truth in the storm's strong sway?
Will you raise your branches high to praise Me for the Son?
Find in Me all your delight until the day is done?

Let your heart be My house I am building for My glory
Let your life be like a book telling redemptions story
Can you help Me be a bridge spanning death's dark waters?
Will you help lead to the gate—earth's lost sons and daughters?

July 24, 2018

Psalm 1:1-3—"Blessed is the one who does not walk in step with the wicked or stand in the way that sinners take or sit in the company of mockers, ² but whose delight is in the law of the Lord, and who meditates on his law day and night. ³ *That person is like a tree* planted by streams of water, which yields its fruit in season and whose leaf does not wither—whatever they do prospers."

Matthew 7:15-23
Psalm 92:12-15
Jeremiah 17:7-8
John 10:7-10

Great is Your Faithfulness

A new day dawns, yet another chance
To change my direction and choose repentance
My spirit is willing, but my flesh is weak
My hope is in You as Your Presence I seek

Great is Your faithfulness, it is new every day
To those who seek to follow and walk in Your "Way"
This Highway of Holiness is narrow and straight
To enter this road, you must go through the gate

"Yes, I am the Way, the Truth and the Life
You have fellowship with Me as you walk in the light
Confess your sins daily I am faithful and just
I will purify your hearts from earth's clinging dust"

"No one comes to the Father except through Me
Those who obey Me are the ones who will see
On that great Day, your bodies will rise
To join the cloud of witnesses high up in the skies"

August 14, 2017

Lamentations 3:22-23—"Because of the LORD's great love we are not consumed, for his compassions never fail. ^{23} They are new every morning; great is your faithfulness."

Lamentations 3
Isaiah 36:8-10
Matthew 7:13-14
John 14:6-21

1 John 1:5-10
Hebrews 12:1-13

    When I read of the martyrs who went before me and loved the Lord more than their lives, I am filled with wonder. How can I hope to die for the Lord when I find it hard to live for the Lord?

Reclaim the Treasure

Look deep within the caverns, of your innermost being
The Holy Spirit lights the way to what you will be seeing
You will find forgotten treasure—stored there long ago
Be quick to search and understand, those things that you must know

I've taught you much these many years, it's easy to forget
You now are dull of hearing, and all your ways are set
Look deep within your heart, see truth and wisdom there
Reclaim the treasure hidden deep, worth much and very rare

When you search with all your heart, My Presence you will find
I am Truth and Wisdom, a River of Life divine
Do not fear, I beckon you, come drink and have your fill
I will teach you, by My Spirit, from My Holy Hill

March 5, 2019

Psalm 24:3-6—"Who may ascend the mountain of the LORD? Who may stand in his holy place? *4* The one who has clean hands and a pure heart, who does not trust in an idol or swear by a false god. *5* They will receive blessing from the LORD and vindication from God their Savior. *6* Such is the generation of those who seek him, who seek your face, God of Jacob."

Revelation 2:1-7
John 4:9-14
John 7:37-39

Kingdom Unity

The kingdom of God is made up of many peoples
They've created different churches under similar looking steeples
I do not have many bodies, there is only one
They are part of Me, and the bride of My dear Son

Each one is a different piece of a puzzle large
Each one has a unique message I've gifted them to charge
There is not one individual more important than the rest
When one of them is missing, My concern is manifest

The picture of My puzzle cannot be seen until complete
All will be made clear at the foot of My judgment seat
Eternal gates will open as each person enters glory
My body joined together will form a wondrous story

January 26, 2019

John 17:22-23—" I have given them the glory that you gave me, that they may be one as we are one— **23** I in them and you in me—so that they may be brought to complete unity. Then the world will know that you sent me and have loved them even as you have loved me."

John 17:20-26
1 Corinthians 12
Ephesians 4:1-16

Eternity in Our Hearts

No man can perceive the future, or what is to come
Who can know their day of death, or its yearly sum?
No one has the power to retain their spirit on that day
The ultimate destination of each one—God has the final say

None can comprehend His works—all that God has done
There is a time for everything that is done under the sun
I asked my God for wisdom, to know Him and His ways
So that I may live in His favor for all my earthly days

Remember your Creator, before the days of trouble come
When your tired old body, has worn out its earthly welcome
Ancient gates will open, revealing every hidden thing
God will bring to judgment, the deeds of every human being

God has set eternity in the hearts of men
Yet they cannot fathom the beginning and the end
Each life is a test, proved true by many fires
Did we live for God, or just selfish desires?

Things done in this life, will matter for all eternity
Treasures earned down here, will reside in that great city
You will know, as you are known, with mercy in each eye
Eternity will then reveal, each where, each what, each why

January 7, 2019

Ecclesiastes 3:9-11—"What does the worker gain from his toil? [10] I have seen the burden God has laid on men. [11] He has made everything beautiful in its time. He has also set eternity in the hearts of men; yet they cannot fathom what God has done from beginning to end."

Ecclesiastes 3:17—"I said to myself, "God will bring into judgment both the righteous and the wicked, for there will be a time for every activity, a time to judge every deed."

Ecclesiastes chapters 3, 8, 12

    I asked the Lord one morning, "What will eternity be like?" It is hard for me to understand not only where will we be during this time, but what will we be doing for all eternity? As I was waiting to hear an answer, Ecclesiastes eight and twelve came to my mind, so I read and meditated on those chapters. This poem soon followed.

Only a Miracle Will Do

There are times when only a miracle will do
For those who have trusted and believed in You
The wait has been long, the oppression so strong
Please come and deliver those whom to You belong

Send oil for healing, with hope intervene
As Your angels tenderly minister behind the scene
Release faith to access Your storehouse above
Fill Your loved ones on earth with mercy and love

Job did not know the reason for his suffering and pain
He endured to the end and received double gain
He was a man who believed and did much good
In suffering his eyes were opened and he understood

One day we will know the reasons of all we go through
But now is the time when only a miracle will do
Release healings and wonders from Your storehouse above
To those waiting below with faith, hope and love

March 26, 2018

Psalm 77:14—"You are the God who performs miracles; you display your power among the peoples."

Hebrews 1:14
Job 1 & 2
Job 42:1-5

    When I awoke in the middle of the night, I couldn't sleep, so I started praying for people. My friend Grace came to mind. She had endured many years of blindness and was also greatly handicapped in her body. She is a Godly woman and trusts in the Lord. I have never given up praying for a miracle for her—for her body to be totally restored. As long as there is life, there is hope. As I was praying for her, this poem came to me.

    Join with me in praying for a miracle in your life, for health, bad situations, or loved ones. This poem is our prayer.

Like Grass in a Field

Life is so short, like grass in a field
Under scorching sun, its beauty does yield
One day it is flourishing, but the next season gone
The landscape has changed, the Lord's favor withdrawn

Ask for the rains to return to the land
Awake the dormant grass and its territory expand
The skies will seem dark, but as the rain falls
Life will return and its beauty enthrall

Awake oh my soul and wait patiently for Him
Let life giving waters fill my hope to the brim
My delight is in the Lord and in Him do I trust
He will not forsake us for the Lord loves the just

September 27, 2017

James 5:17-18—"Elijah was a human being, even as we are. He prayed earnestly that it would not rain, and it did not rain on the land for three and a half years. [18] Again he prayed, and the heavens gave rain, and the earth produced its crops."

Isaiah 37:27
Haggai 1:7-11
Psalm 37

    I got this poem during a time of unusual weather for Pittsburgh. It is usually rainy here in the fall. But it had been very hot and sunny for two weeks, and the forecast called for at least ten more days of this weather. I saw how brown the grass was getting. This poem then came to mind.

CHAPTER 3

Come Up Higher

Ascending Steps into the Temple—Come Up Higher

Leaving the sea and heading to the Temple, there were ascending stairs that led to the Temple doors. This conveys the idea we need to come up higher to enter the Holy Place. Revelation 4:1-2 shows us a door standing open in heaven and a voice entreating John to "come up here, and I will show you what must take place." This speaks of revelation knowledge given to those who are desiring to lead a holy life. It is in our ascending spiritually we find that circumstances are working to lower and humble ourselves causing us to die to self. That is what it will cost us to enter the Holy Place, but it will be worth everything we have to be in that special place. If you are desiring this—Come Up Higher.

Come Up Higher

Come up here, I want to show you many things
You'll find yourself soaring, as if you had wings
The door is now open, I invite you to draw near
Experience My love, it will cast out all your fear

Clothe yourself with compassion for the weak and the lost
Spend yourself for others and do not count the cost
Did you notice those suffering as you passed quickly by?
I will show you who to stop for, and guide you by My eye

Walk in forgiveness and do not harden your heart
Obedience and the fear of the Lord is the place to start
Draw near; take your shoes off, for this is holy ground
Worship in My Presence—there, grace and mercy abound

Come up higher, new realms of glory you will find
Here you'll receive gifts, new hearts, and new minds
I give you grace to draw near, to know Me and My ways
Now go back and share with others for all of your days

October 19, 2018

Revelation 4:1, 2—"After this I looked, and there before me was a door standing open in heaven. And the voice I had first heard speaking to me like a trumpet said, "Come up here, and I will show you what must take place after this." ² At once I was in the Spirit, and there before me was a throne in heaven with someone sitting on it."

1 John 4:7-21
Matthew 6:14-15

Matthew 18:21-35
Ephesians 4:20-24
Ezekiel 36:22-27

The City Up Above

I'm longing for that city—the heavenly one above
Whose builder is the Lord—whose canopy is love
No fear will stalk its sidewalks, no stranger dwells therein
Only safety, peace and harmony accompany each citizen

Abraham saw this city, from a distance, and his heart did yearn
By faith he traveled like a stranger on a long sojourn
He obeyed and went, and lived in tents, in a foreign land
Always trusting his great God, even when he didn't understand

John had a revelation of this city coming from above
Its holy radiance descended from the sky, gentle as a dove
Like a bride, dressed in jewels, its sparkling brilliance shown
All those waiting for Jesus, its residence will own

"Come, take My hand and follow Me, only I know the way
I'll lead you to this Promised Land if on the path you'll stay
This wilderness you're traveling through, you'll learn to trust "The Three"
The greatest treasure you can gain, is to be found in Me"

"Do not despise this perilous desert you now are traveling through
It's where you'll learn to trust Me, and know My ways are true
Heavenly treasures are hidden there to enjoy and collect without measure
This wilderness journey will reveal—I am the greatest treasure"

July 2, 2018

Revelation 21:2-3—"I saw the Holy City, the new Jerusalem, coming down out of heaven from God, prepared as a bride beautifully dressed for her husband. ³ And I heard a loud voice from the throne saying, "Look! God's dwelling place is now among the people, and he will dwell with them. They will be his people, and God himself will be with them and be their God."

Hebrews 11:8-16
Revelation 21 & 22
1 Corinthians 10:1-13

The Treasures of a Heart

Things of great value have a great price you must pay
The cost isn't always money on its price tag display
Who can put an amount on the treasures of a heart?
Who can claim its riches or its benefits impart?

It is I, the Lord, who searches out its hidden worth
By My Spirit and circumstances, its treasures I unearth
You say, "I am rich and do not need a thing"
But you don't realize who is pulling your heart string

I counsel you to buy from Me gold refined in fire
So you can become rich, then make Me your desire
Please hear Me knocking, I'm standing at the door
"Invite Me in for fellowship," I lovingly implore

Rise up with faith, to conquer in My name
Believe in My promises with your soul set aflame
Then I will invite you to sit with Me, on My throne
Examine your heart now to see what treasures you own

October 1, 2018

Psalm 139:23-24—"Search me, God, and know my heart; test me and know my anxious thoughts. [24] See if there is any offensive way in me, and lead me in the way everlasting."

Romans 8:27
Revelation 3:14-22
Matthew 6:19-33

Seek My Glory

Seek My glory and My grace—there mercy does abide
Do everything for My Name's sake, let My Spirit to be your guide
In the light of My celestial glory, all other glories fade
You are only earthen vessels that the heavenly Potter made

I dwell in the midst of your praises, and hear all you say
Your words are bound in books to be revealed on that "Day"
Then your motives will be laid bare for everyone to see
Did you seek glory for yourself or seek only to please Me?

Judge yourselves now and repent, before it's too late
It will not be very long till you stand before Heaven's Gate
The only sacrifice accepted will be My blood shed for thee
If you believe this in your heart, then you will share in My glory

Seek My glory, become transformed, then be made anew
Only then will you find selfless motivations that are true
When you search for My abiding Presence, with all of your heart
My love will dwell in you and My radiant fullness I will impart

Seek only My resplendent glory and not from one another
How empty and meaningless to seek praise from each other
Look at Me with unveiled faces and My Presence then will shine
You'll be transformed into My likeness, with rapturous glory divine

August 6, 2018

2 Corinthians 3:18—"And we all, who with unveiled faces reflect the Lord's glory, are being transformed into his image with ever-increasing glory, which comes from the Lord, who is the Spirit."

Malachi 3:16-18
John 11:40
John 17:20 -26
Romans 2: 6-11
Romans 8:16-18
Colossians 1:24-27
2 Corinthian's 3:12-18

    I woke up in the middle of the night and the words, "Seek My Glory," popped into my thoughts. The next morning, I looked up in the concordance the word 'glory' and studied those passages. Some of them I have listed above. Then, the weekly email from Francis Frangipane arrived in my inbox titled "Find God." It was so good I had to include it here.

Holiness Comes from Seeking the Glory of God
    Jesus warned, "How can you believe, when you receive glory from one another, and you do not seek the glory that is from the one and only God?" (John 5:44). If we are displaying our spirituality to impress men, still seeking honor from others, still living to appear righteous or special or "anointed" before people, can we honestly say we have been walking near to the living God? We know we are relating correctly to God when our hunger for His glory causes us to forsake the praise of men.

Does not all glory fade in the light of His glory? Even as Jesus challenged the genuineness of the Pharisees' faith, so He challenges us: "How can you believe, when you receive glory from one another?"

What a weak comfort is the praise of men. Upon such a frail ledge do we mortals build our happiness. Consider: within but a few days after the Lycaonians attempted to *worship* Paul, they were congratulating themselves for having stoned him (Acts 14:11-19). Consider: was it not the same city whose songs and praise welcomed Jesus as "King…gentle, and mounted on a donkey" (Matt. 21:5-9) that roared, "Crucify Him!" less than one week later (Luke 23:21)? To seek the praise of men is to be tossed upon such a sea of instability!

We must ask ourselves, whose glory do we seek in life, God's or our own? Jesus said, "He who speaks from himself seeks his own glory" (John 7:18). When we speak from ourselves and of ourselves, are we not seeking to solicit from men the praise that belongs only to God? To seek our glory is to fall headlong into vanity and deception. "But," Jesus continued, "He who is seeking the glory of the one who sent Him, He is true and there is no unrighteousness in Him." (v. 18) The same quality of heart that made Christ's intentions true must become our standard as well. *For only to the degree that we are seeking the glory of God are our motivations true! Only to the degree that we abide in the glory of Him who sends us is there no unrighteousness in our hearts!*

Therefore, let us give ourselves to seeking the glory of God, and let us do so until we find Him. As we behold the nature of Christ, as our eyes see *Him*, like Job we "abhor" ourselves and "repent in dust and ashes" (Job 42:6 KJV). As we are bathed in His glory, we shall be washed from seeking the glory of man.

If we truly find Him, no one will have to tell us to be humble. No one need convince us our old natures are as filthy rags. As we truly find God, the things which are so highly esteemed among men will become detestable in our sight (Luke 16:15).

What could be more important than finding God? Take a day, a week or a month and do nothing but seek Him, persisting until you find Him. He has promised, "You will seek Me and find Me, when you search for Me with all your heart (Jer. 29:13)." Find God, and once you have Him, determine to live the rest of your life in pursuit of His glory. As you touch Him, something will come alive in you: something eternal, someone Almighty! Instead of looking down on people, you will seek to lift them up. You will dwell in the presence of God. And you will be holy, for *He* is holy.

Adapted from Francis Frangipane's book, *Holiness, Truth and the Presence of God*, available at www.arrowbookstore.com. Used with permission.

Love's Quest

Me:
Help me to walk in the light of Your love
To be wise as a serpent, but harmless as a dove
Clothed in Your glory, I will see through Your eyes
I'll see past their mask, they wear as a disguise

Lord:
I'll join you in love's quest as we journey down life's road
To help those you encounter, bent down under life's heavy load
Weary, forgotten, they stumble along, all alone
With tears in His eyes, the Father sees from His throne

This is My command—that you love each other well
Laying down your life, to help save people from hell
You are My friends, if you do what I command
Love is the fulfillment of the Law's demand

Love's quest is a journey that leads to heaven's door
Those who walk that road receive joy forevermore
Glory unspeakable, untold riches await those
Who lay down their lives and dress in love's clothes

January 2, 2019

John 17:20-23 - "My prayer is not for them alone. I pray also for those who will believe in me through their message, [21] that all of them may be one, Father, just as you are in me and I am in you. May they also be in us so that the world may believe that you have sent me. [22] *I have given them the glory that you gave me, that they may be one as we are one—* [23] I in them and you in me—so that they may be brought to complete unity. Then the world will know that you sent me and have loved them even as you have loved me."

Colossians 3:12-14—"Therefore, as God's chosen people, holy and dearly loved, *clothe yourselves with compassion, kindness, humility, gentleness and patience.* [13] Bear with each other and forgive one another if any of you has a grievance against someone. Forgive as the Lord forgave you.[14] *And over all these virtues put on love, which binds them all together in perfect unity.*"

John 15:9-17
Matthew 10:16 KJV
1 John 2:3-11
1 John 3:1-24
Ephesians 4:22-24

As I sat in my devotion time pondering the New Year ahead of me, I wondered what lay ahead of me in the coming months. I felt like the Lord's message to me was, "…to walk in love." I knew I needed the Lord's help for that, then, this poem came to me as my prayer, and the Lord's reply to that prayer.

Love Has Won

Stay connected to Me throughout each passing day
Discern My loving Presence as you walk along the way
Talk to Me as though I'm standing close beside you
Speak forth in faith, because My promises are true

To those around you who need healing, stretch forth your hand
I've given you authority, so speak out your command
The powers of hell will flee at the sound of your voice
Contested ground won, causing saints to rejoice

The battle belongs not to the strong, but to those—
Who choose Me and My ways, and dress in love's clothes
Let the fruit of the Spirit be your strength and your shield
As you bring in the harvest from the enemy's captured field

The kingdoms of this world will become the kingdom of My Son
Victory over darkness will prove love has won
The King will be crowned in the throne room on high
Every knee will then bow and every tongue testify

January 29, 2019

Philippians 2:8-11—"And being found in appearance as a man, he humbled himself and became obedient to death—even death on a cross! [9] Therefore God exalted him to the highest place and gave him the name that is above every name, [10] that at the name of Jesus every knee should bow, in heaven and on earth and under the earth, [11] and every tongue confess that Jesus Christ is Lord, to the glory of God the Father."

Job 29:14—"I put on righteousness as my clothing; justice was my robe and my turban."

Deuteronomy 6:1-12
Colossians 3:12-14
Galatians 5:22-25
Revelation 11:15-19
Psalm 45:1-7

*"…..His kingdom grows more through the patient bearing of fruit than through attacking the works of the devil. There is a time for attacking the strongholds of the devil, but that is never the main work of the kingdom." From, "The Torch and the Sword," by Rick Joyner, page 103.

* "The Torch and the Sword," by Rick Joyner. Copywrite 2003. Used by permission www.morningstarministries.org

Prophet Without Honor

Only in his hometown is a prophet without honor
Questioning the source, is what many are left to ponder
Whatever is the message, they are quick to inspect
They are looking to find fault so they can smugly reject

Jesus, in His hometown synagogue, stood up to read
Turning to Isaiah, He read of prisoners freed
"I am sent to give blind sight and good news to the poor"
But, instead of giving honor, they kicked Him out the door

If they did this to Him, what can we expect?
No matter what the message, those closest might reject
When the Spirit is poured out, dreams and visions will go forth
It will take much courage, to follow Him thenceforth

This will serve to humble those, sent to do His will
Not to walk in fear of man or earthly desires fulfill
The way of Jesus is the cross; we must follow to the end
Then we'll hear those precious words, "You are not My servant, but My friend"

March 12, 2019

Mark 6:4—"Jesus said to them, "A prophet is not without honor except in his own town, among his relatives and in his own home."

Mark 6:1-6
Luke 4:14-30

In following the Lord, we should never let discouragement over what we are going through rule over us. Sometimes, those events are the very tools God uses to refine us and our desires, and yes, even to humble us. It is in submitting ourselves to God's will we can accept dishonor, rebuke and setbacks. Indeed, what seems like a setback, can, in God's hands, become a setup for a greater victory. There are many examples of that in the Bible.

It is because God closed doors in my life to teach that I thought to write a book. If my desire to teach had been fulfilled, I would never have had the time to write.

As you exercise your faith and trust in Him for direction, He can turn your setbacks into a setup that releases you to your destiny.

In Him Do I Trust

Not in the strength of horses do I feel secure
Nor is it by my wealth that I hope to endure
The Lord alone—in Him do I trust
For the eyes of God watch over the just

"As the bird in the tree watches from on high
Or surveys its domain as it glides in the sky
So do I keep watch on My loved ones below
Supplying their needs while into My likeness they grow"

Oh, taste and see that the Lord is truly good
Learn the fear of the Lord under His Fatherhood
The righteous may have many troubles and fall
But the Lord will deliver him from them all

November 23, 2017

Isaiah 31:1—"Woe to those who go down to Egypt for help, who rely on horses, who trust in the multitude of their chariots and in the great strength of their horsemen, but do not look to the Holy One of Israel, or seek help from the Lord."

2 Chronicles 16:7-9
Psalm 34

Embrace the New

Get rid of the old so you can embrace the new
Clean out the closets, it's much overdue
A new day is dawning, arise at the light
Search for My Presence, make Me your delight

Set your heart on the path that only I know
As you step forth in faith, My grace I'll bestow
You can't travel this journey weighted down with things
As you lighten the load, you'll soar with new wings

I've placed desires in your heart I'm longing to fill
Come into My Presence, wait, and be still
Your ears will hear a voice saying, "This is the way"
Let's go forth together, do not delay

The hour is late, there is work to be done
You need not hold back, I am your provision
My Spirit accompanies My Word with great power
A new age is coming, you were born for this hour

September 3, 2018

Psalm 37:4—"Take delight in the Lord, and he will give you the desires of your heart."

Isaiah 42:9
Ephesians 4:17-32
Ephesians 5:8-21
Isaiah 30:18-22
Ephesians 2:6-10

I had wanted to clean out my closet for some time and get rid of things I wasn't using anymore. The morning, I finally got started, this poem came to me.

Undivided Heart

Me:
Give me a heart to know Your ways
My desire is to follow You all of my days
Remove from me a heart of stone
Replace it with love for You alone

A kingdom divided cannot stand
Uncover hidden idols throughout the land
Give to me an undivided heart
A healing balm will Your Spirit impart

Lord:
Return to Me and I will return to you
I'll send blessings from heaven with the morning dew
Restoring to you what the enemy has taken
You will be found with My likeness, when you awaken

Peace, peace, will then alight upon you
In My Presence all things are made new
Purpose in your heart to follow till the end
New life awaits you, My bride, My friend

June 5, 2019

Psalm 86:11—"Teach me your way, Lord, that I may rely on your faithfulness; give me an undivided heart, that I may fear your name."

Psalm 17:15—"As for me, I will be vindicated and will see your face; when I awake, I will be satisfied with seeing your likeness."

Jeremiah 24:7
Jeremiah 32:36-41
Ezekiel 11:16-21
James 4:1-10

CHAPTER 4

God is Light

The Lampstand—God is Light

Upon entering the Temple doors, the lampstand was one of the first things you would have seen. The purpose of the lampstand or menorah was to give light and to show that God is Light because it represented His Presence. Just as light reveals dark and hidden things, so the Light of God reveals mysteries and things hidden by darkness. It is in the Light of His Presence that we can see the wounds on His body that Jesus suffered for us. He also asks us to join in His suffering with Him, just as He told the apostle Paul at the beginning of his ministry that he would have to suffer many things for the sake of the gospel. Jesus proclaimed Himself to be the light of the world in John 8:12. In saying this He was claiming to be God because—God is Light.

God is Light

The light of God went forth, even before time began
In Him there is no darkness, throughout eternity's span
Radiating beams of His glory, illuminate heaven's hall
God is light; in His Presence, there is no darkness at all

Mysteries abound, around this unapproachable light
He made darkness His covering, to hide Himself from our sight
At the dawn of creation, His light already existed
God then called it forth, to banish darkness that persisted

The Spirit of God hovered over the face of the deep
Separating the darkness and gathering it in a heap
He called the light day, the darkness He called night
Evening and morning appeared to the wondering angels' delight

There will be a day, when earth's light will no longer shine
The new heavens and earth will glow, with God's glory divine
Then the light of God that existed, even before time began
Will replace earth's dark shadows and surround every blessed man

February 25, 2019

1 John 1:5—"This is the message we have heard from him and declare to you: God is light; in him there is no darkness at all."

Genesis 1:1-5—"In the beginning God created the heavens and the earth. ² Now the earth was formless and empty, darkness was over the surface of the deep, and the Spirit of God was hovering over the waters."

³And God said, "Let there be light," and there was light. ⁴God saw that the light was good, and he separated the light from the darkness.⁵ God called the light "day," and the darkness he called "night." And there was evening, and there was morning—the first day.

1 Timothy 6:16
John 11:9
Psalm 18:9-11
Job 38:1-21
Revelation 21:1-5, 22-27

Fill My Lamp

Oh Lord, let me be done, with desiring worldly things
Open my heart to the message, the Holy Spirit brings
Let oil fall from heaven, to fill my flickering lamp
I wait to hear Your voice, in the morning dew's chill damp

Fill my mind with visions, to direct and guide my feet
Dreams of possibilities, of those I'm yet to meet
Show wonders in the heavens, and signs on earth below
Pour out Your Spirit, and on us gifts bestow

Only You have words of eternal life, fill my lamp to the brim
Let Your truth guide me in the night, where other lights grow dim
Soon, deep darkness will cover the earth; the Son will hide His face
Because they will reject His Word and spurn His love and grace

A light will arise, like the spreading of dawn, for the entire world to see
Nations will be drawn, by the glory of this dawn, to the Lord's brilliancy
A glorious new age will then appear, behold—there will be no more night
For the glory of the Lord, rising upon you, will be your everlasting light

December 11, 2018

Isaiah 60:1-3 - "Arise, shine, for your light has come, and the glory of the Lord rises upon you.

² See, darkness covers the earth and thick darkness is over the peoples, but the Lord rises upon you and his glory appears over you."

³ "Nations will come to your light, and kings to the brightness of your dawn."

Matthew 25:1-9
Acts 2:14-21
John 6:68-69
Isaiah 60

Give Me Oil

Lord, blow upon the embers that are dying in my heart
Ignite a flame to dancing, causing praise to start
Worldly cares have dampened, a roaring blazing fire
Causing me to lose my holy passion and desire

Holy Spirit, give me oil, to keep the flame alive
Night's dark shadows drive away, so my spirit can revive
Wake me up from slumber deep, to hear the Bridegroom's voice
In the nearness of His coming, I start to rejoice

Give me wisdom to prepare, for that special day
Grant me patience in the night, at the long delay
Let my eyes be watchful, for Your swift return
To be always ready, is my main concern

When at trumpet's final call, my spirit starts to rise
I'll be prepared and ready, to join You in the skies
Then at last we'll be together, never more to part
Reigning from on high, with the Lover of my heart

June 14, 2019

Matthew 25:4-10—"The wise ones, however, took oil in jars along with their lamps. [5] The bridegroom was a long time in coming, and they all became drowsy and fell asleep. [6] "At midnight the cry rang out: "Here's the bridegroom! Come out to meet him!' [7] "Then all the virgins woke up and trimmed their lamps. [8] The foolish ones said to the wise, 'Give us some of your oil; our lamps are going out.' [9] "No,' they replied, 'there may not be enough for both us and you. Instead, go to those who sell oil and buy some for yourselves.' **10** "But while they were on their way to buy the oil, the bridegroom arrived. The virgins who were ready went in with him to the wedding banquet. And the door was shut."

Matthew 25:1-13
2 Corinthians 11:1-2
Titus 2:11-15
2 Peter 3:10-18
1 Thessalonians 4:13-18

Night's Dark Testing

Night's dark testing, is sent to prove our faith
It goes beyond just feeling—to —"the Lord saith"
Our obedience rises up to touch the Father's heart
The Holy Spirit descends with His power to impart

In night's dark testing, I've failed again and again
The moon hides its face because of my transgression
I thought, maybe the darkness, would conceal the offense
But the Lord exposes all so I can be brought to repentance

Because of night's dark testing, I've tried to cover the pain
But the remedy dulls enjoyment, so what did I gain?
Life isn't truly living with all my feelings removed
If I walk this way through life, what was thereby proved?

Joy comes in the morning, after night's dark testing
If I've made right choices, I'll be found in Him resting
When dawn's light beams through the window of my soul
I'll be raised, on that day, with a body incorruptible

February 1, 2019

Psalm 30:4-5(NKJV)—"Sing praise to the Lord, you saints of His, and give thanks at the remembrance of His holy name. ⁵ For His anger *is but for* a moment, His favor *is for* life; weeping may endure for a night, but joy *comes* in the morning."

Job 19:25-27—"I know that my redeemer lives, and that in the end, he will stand on the earth.

²⁶ And after my skin has been destroyed, yet in my flesh I will see God; ²⁷ I myself will see him with my own eyes—I, and not another. How my heart yearns within me!"

Psalm 30
Job 3, 19, 42

The Holocaust

The spirit that influenced Hamon, is alive and well
Its power is derived from the pit of hell
The beloved sons of Israel are the target of its attack
Propaganda spewed has nothing to do with facts

Grief upon grief was in the Lord's whispered voice
Like a lamb to the slaughter, there was no given choice
"Look at what they have done to My son," I heard Him say
As He gazed at the murdered bodies lying on display

The fires of the Holocaust cannot erase this nation
Up from the ashes arose a resurrected habitation
Israel returned to the land of their youth
Free to choose their destiny, free to choose the truth

Rejected by the nations, but chosen of the Lord
Arose a mighty army with a powerful sword
They will by My people, and I will be their God
I choose to dwell among them forever on earth's sod

November 3, 2017

Exodus 4:22-23—"Then say to Pharaoh, 'This is what the LORD says: Israel is my firstborn son, [23] and I told you, "Let my son go, so he may worship me." But you refused to let him go; so I will kill your firstborn son.'"

Esther 3
Ezekiel 37
Ezekiel 43:1-7
Jeremiah 31

My friend Margie and I went to Washington D.C. at the end of October 2017 to visit some popular sites. We decided to visit the Holocaust Museum the next day, and as I contemplated on the sad sights awaiting us, a scene from the movie "The Godfather" came into my mind. As the Godfather was delivering his sons bloody bullet-ridden body to the undertaker, I saw him say, "Look at what they did to my son." (In the movie, the actual quote from the Godfather to the undertaker was mumbled, but I think he said, "Look how they messed with my boy.") I knew as I was watching this play in my mind, the Lord was saying the same thing to me about His son, Israel, "Look at what they did to my son." I remembered that saying the next day as I toured the museum and felt the Lord's grief as I saw all those murdered bodies. Over the next few days, this poem came to me.

The High Road of Holiness

The high road of holiness leads to realms of glory
Eternity will thrill as each recount their story
The things we've learned on earth will follow us forever
Perfected understanding will bind our hearts together

Only the redeemed can walk upon this road
Its final destination leads to God's abode
Jesus went ahead to prepare a place for us
In Him is our life and in His ways we trust

Jesus, our Lord, is the way, the truth and the life
Clashes against darkness produce much pain and strife
If we walk in the light, He will illuminate the way
Darkness must flee at the approaching bright day

This "Way of Holiness" is narrow and straight
The only access is through Jesus the gate
Gladness and joy will overtake those on that "Way"
As darkness recedes into never ending day

March 6, 2018

Isaiah 35:8—"And a highway will be there; it will be called the Way of Holiness; it will be for those who walk on that Way. The unclean will not journey on it; wicked fools will not go about on it."

Hebrews 12:14—"Make every effort to live in peace with everyone and to be holy; without holiness no one will see the Lord."

Isaiah 35
John 14:1-14
1 John 1:5-10
John 10:7-10

The Path of Life

You tend to go where the eye does lead
Focused on earthly desires you pick up much more speed
Going faster down the road you can quickly leave the path of life
Till all of a sudden, you are lost, and cannot find the light

"Lord, how did I get here?" Is the question you might say
"Lord, how can I return?" Is the prayer you must pray
In singleness of heart, let your eye be turned upon Me
I will give you sound direction, and with wisdom you will see

You are not alone; I will join you on life's road
Yolk yourself with Me, I will help you with life's load
Live by the Spirit, walk in step with the Holy One
He will lead you to heaven's glory when earthly days are done

December 22, 2018

Psalm 16:11—"You make known to me the path of life; you will fill me with joy in your presence, with eternal pleasures at your right hand."

Matthew 11:28-30—"Come to me, all you who are weary and burdened, and I will give you rest. ²⁹ Take my yoke upon you and learn from me, for I am gentle and humble in heart, and you will find rest for your souls. ³⁰ For my yoke is easy and my burden is light."

Job 31:1-8
Proverbs 2
Galatians 5

Sent to Deceive

You will be seeing things you do not understand
Know I allow these things; they all come from My hand
Monsters and mysteries released upon the earth
Sent to deceive those, who do not have the rebirth

I allow the mist to part, so that some may catch a glimpse
They do not understand they are seeing devilish imps
Their fear is but a foretaste of the hell that does wait
For those who reject Me—eternal torment is their fate

"Can their destiny be changed?" Is the question you might ask
For the hardened in heart, the face they wear is a mask
Their dirty soul within, runs and hides from the light
Because they refuse to hear, and do what is right

My faithful will see the truth and hear My Word come alive
If you follow My Spirit closely, you will not have to strive
My angels go with you, to guide and to protect
Follow close behind Me—be sure My Word you respect

February 14, 2019

1 Kings 22:19-23—"Micaiah continued, "Therefore hear the word of the LORD: I saw the LORD sitting on his throne with all the multitudes of heaven standing around him on his right and on his left. [20] And the LORD said, 'Who will entice Ahab into attacking Ramoth Gilead and going to his death there?'

"One suggested this, and another that. [21] Finally, a spirit came forward, stood before the LORD and said, 'I will entice him.'

²² "'By what means?' the Lord asked. "'I will go out and be a deceiving spirit in the mouths of all his prophets,' he said. 'You will succeed in enticing him,' said the Lord. 'Go and do it.' ²³ "So now the Lord has put a deceiving spirit in the mouths of all these prophets of yours. The Lord has decreed disaster for you."

Zachariah 4:6—"So he said to me, "This is the word of the Lord to Zerubbabel: 'Not by might nor by power, but by my Spirit,' says the Lord Almighty."

Revelation 9:1-21
1 John 1:5-10

Obedience Learned

Me:
I want to hear Your voice, oh Lord, that is my desire
Fill me with the Spirit's oil, my flickering lamp re-fire
Keep pouring till I'm filled with love, for lost humanity
Obedience learned, leads to fruit, from the tree of charity

Lord:
Eat your fill, My tender dove, from this most desirable fruit
Crucify the sinful nature and make Me your passionate pursuit
Come, sit under the shade I provide, and rest your weary soul
Learn from Me and My ways, My beloved, for I am meek and merciful

If you love Me, obey My commands, with a cheerful heart
You cannot do this in your own strength, so My Spirit I will impart
Obedience learned, by the things you suffer, is a treasure rare
An attitude of reverent submission is an acceptable and sacrificial prayer

Do not desire to hear My voice, unless you fully commit
Follow closely, obey My words, and to My ways, submit
The way may be hard and filled with pain, by following My perfect will
But eternity will prove, the reward will be great, for obedience fulfilled

January 12, 2019

Hebrews 5:7-9—"During the days of Jesus' life on earth, he offered up prayers and petitions with fervent cries and tears to the one who could save him from death, and he was heard because of his reverent submission. **8** Son though he was, he learned obedience from what he suffered **9** and, once made perfect, he became the source of eternal salvation for all who obey him."

Galatians 5:22-26
Song of Songs 2:3-6
Matthew 11:28-30

Unfading Beauty

Passion and desire, is what beauty reaps
Igniting a quick flame, that burns in lovers deep
The way of a man, beholds a maiden fair
Then he is held captive by her eyes and her hair

Eventually beauty fades, desire grows weak
Wisdom and understanding searches out the meek
If we allow the virtue of God, to become our dress
We'll then seek His face, and ask Him our ways to bless

The way of a man, judges by what he sees
Our righteous God, considers our hearts qualities
God is light—a consuming searching ray
Exposing in His light, beauty, dust, decay

Welcome this purifying beam of God that exposes all
It releases grace and mercy on all who call
When strolling on Heaven's streets of gold, we finally will see
Each other through God's eyes of love—glorious, unfading beauty

March 18, 2019

Proverbs 30:18-19—"There are three things that are too amazing for me, four that I do not understand: ¹⁹ the way of an eagle in the sky, the way of a snake on a rock, the way of a ship on the high seas, and the way of a man with a young woman."

1 Samuel 16:7—"But the LORD said to Samuel, "Do not consider his appearance or his height, for I have rejected him.

The LORD does not look at the things people look at. People look at the outward appearance, but the LORD looks at the heart."

Song of Songs 7:1-6
Ecclesiastes 12

In my half- awakened state one morning, I thought of how beauty fades over time and because of it sometimes lovers drift apart. "Does beauty fade in heaven?" My searching mind asked the Lord. As I searched scriptures, this poem came to my mind.

Quench Not My Spirit

Quench not My Spirit and put out My holy fire
Do not assume direction until you seek Me and inquire
My ways are hidden from the world, lest they see and hear
You must learn to ask and wait, with an obedient, listening ear

The busyness of life drowns out the Holy Spirit's voice
When you clearly hear from Me, don't treat it as a choice
Better not to hear at all, than hear and then refuse
Eternal destinies will result--from whose voice you choose

Is not My Word like fire, sent to burn away the dross?
Yes, it will be painful, to go the way of the cross
Ask for My Holy Spirit, to baptize you with fire
As the tongues of flames descend, you'll be filled with His desires

Do not quench My Holy Spirit--let Him guide you along the way
His fire will light dark paths that lead to never-ending day
Then battles will be over, the victor's crown be won
You'll thrill to hear this greeting—"Well done My faithful son"

February 2, 2019

Jeremiah 20:9—"But if I say, "I will not mention his word or speak anymore in his name," his word is in my heart like a fire, a fire shut up in my bones. I am weary of holding it in; indeed, I cannot."

Jeremiah 23:29—"Is not my word like fire," declares the Lord, "and like a hammer that breaks a rock in pieces?"

Luke 12:49—"I have come to bring fire on the earth, and how I wish it were already kindled!"

1 Thessalonians 5:19-22
Matthew 13:15
Luke 3:15-16
Psalm 39
Acts 2:1-12
Matthew 25:21

A Song of All Songs

Me:
A song of all songs, to the King of all Kings
You alone are worthy of the worship my heart sings
Let the melody of the night, rise to greet You at the dawn
As hope turns into faith, I know You will respond

The passion of the music causes me to dance
The beauty of Your Word speaks of Your longing for romance
Your bride, the church, prepares herself, for that special day
As the radiance of Your glory rises upon her in full array

Lord:
Arise, My love, My beautiful one, and come away with Me
Meet Me as that great day breaks and the shadows flee
All beautiful you are, My love, there is no flaw in you
Arise and join the searching One, whose head is drenched with dew

Do not arouse or awaken love, until it so desires
The times are in My hands—as are refining fires
Be awake and ready, holding high your lamp aglow
When I come to gather you, in earth's darkest night below

December 27, 2018

Song of Songs 7:5-6—"Your head crowns you like Mount Carmel. Your hair is like royal tapestry; the king is held captive by its tresses. ⁶ How beautiful you are and how pleasing, my love, with your delights!"

Song of Songs: read the entire book and take to heart the Lord's love for you

Isaiah 60:1-3
Malachi 3:1-3

CHAPTER 5

Bread of Life

The Table Holding the - Bread of Life

Another article inside the Temple doors in the room called the Holy Place, was a piece of furniture called the Table for the Bread of the Presence. This table held twelve loaves of bread each day for the priests to eat. Jesus said, "He was the bread that came down from heaven," in John 6:58. When we eat bread, it becomes a part of us and remains in us. Just as we need bread every day to nourish our physical bodies, we should be feeding our spirits on the Word of God, for He is the—Bread of Life.

Bread of life

Feed upon My Word, it will strengthen and sustain you
I am the "Bread of Life," appearing like morning dew
I came down from heaven to do My Father's will
All who come to Me, can eat and have their fill

I have spread the table; I wait for you to come
You have been too busy, you find it burdensome
The one who feeds on this bread, will live eternally
Sweet fellowship enjoyed, as you remain in Me

This bread is baked fresh daily and offered now to you
Feed upon My Word, as My direction you pursue
When you eat this bread from heaven, you will never die
Your body raised immortal, will then be glorified

November 26, 2018

John 6:56-58—"Whoever eats my flesh and drinks my blood remains in me, and I in them. ⁵⁷ Just as the living Father sent me and I live because of the Father, so the one who feeds on me will live because of me. ⁵⁸ This is the bread that came down from heaven. Your ancestors ate manna and died, but whoever feeds on this bread will live forever."

John 6:25-69
Exodus 16:4-15
1 Corinthians 11:23-34
Exodus 25:23-30
Leviticus 24:5-9
Romans 8:28-30

Manna's Dew

Come to the table, partake of His Word
Eye has not seen nor has the ear heard
Of all the wondrous mysteries contained within
A revelation of Jesus is to be found therein

God's Word speaks of His love, it speaks of His grace
Each promise longs to hold you in its sure embrace
Dispensing rest for the weary with its life-giving waters
Imparting faith, hope and love to earth's sons and daughters

There is only one truth, only one way
Jesus, God in the flesh, in brilliant display
When we partake of His body and drink communion's cup
He becomes one with us, in fellowship to sup

Just as Israel of old, daily ate manna's dew
So He wants His Word to become a part of you
The one who eats this bread will live eternally
They'll be raised up at the last day with immortality

May 1, 2019

John 1:14—"The Word became flesh and made his dwelling among us. We have seen his glory, the glory of the one and only Son, who came from the Father, full of grace and truth."

John 6:57-58—"Just as the living Father sent me and I live because of the Father, so the one who feeds on me will live because of me. [58] This is the bread that came down from heaven. Your ancestors ate manna and died, but whoever feeds on this bread will live forever."

Exodus 16:13-15, 31—"That evening quail came and covered the camp, and in the morning there was a layer of dew around the camp. ¹⁴ When the dew was gone, thin flakes like frost on the ground appeared on the desert floor. ¹⁵ When the Israelites saw it, they said to each other, "What is it?", for they did not know what it was. Moses said to them, "It is the bread the LORD has given you to eat." 31"The people of Israel called the bread manna. It was white like coriander seed and tasted like wafers made with honey."

John 6:25-59
1 Corinthians 2:6-16
Exodus 16:1-15

Hearing Your Voice

I want to hear Your voice, Oh Lord, more than anything
Wisdom, knowledge, love, and guidance, I'm hoping You will bring
As golden nuggets strewn about, Your Scriptures come to mind
Like treasure hidden in a field, that suddenly I find

Where morning dawns, and evening fades, You call forth songs of joy
I respond with eager heart, Your praises to employ
You crown my year with Your bounty, and hear me when I pray
Answering with awesome deeds, Your glory to display

Let me hear Your voice, Oh Lord, to know You and Your will
As I calm my heart before You, waiting, patient, still
Open up my eyes to see, the issues of Your heart
As I delight myself in You, Your glory, You'll impart

May 25, 2019

Psalm 32:8—"I will instruct you and teach you in the way you should go; I will counsel you with my loving eye on you."

Psalm 25:14—"The LORD confides in those who fear him; he makes his covenant known to them."

Psalm 19
Psalm 50
Psalm 65

Passing Through the Valley

In the presence of my enemies a table is prepared
With choice foods and sweets that can't be compared
"Come dine with Me, stay awhile," I heard the Lord say
"There is a seat at the table beside Me today"

The noise of the day grew swiftly dim
As I got off the path to spend time with Him
I put down those things that distracted and annoyed
And replaced them with hope, peace, love and joy

We sat down to eat in green pastures so fair
By flowing streams lined with trees of apple and pear
"Come dwell in My house at the end of the day
When nights shadows come creeping to take you away"

"You will pass through the valley of the shadow of death
When the enemy comes calling to steal away your breath
But I will be there with My rod and My staff
When the wheat is separated from the grain and the chaff"

"The wind of My Spirit will blow the chaff away
As night recedes into never ending day
At the end of the path is My city so bright
Where My Father and I are its never-ending light"

August 25, 2017

Isaiah 35:8-10—"And a highway will be there; it will be called the Way of Holiness; it will be for those who walk on that Way. The unclean will not journey on it; wicked fools will not go about on it. ⁹ No lion will be there, nor any ravenous beast; they will not be found there. But only the redeemed will walk there,¹⁰ and those the LORD has rescued will return. They will enter Zion with singing; everlasting joy will crown their heads. Gladness and joy will overtake them, and sorrow and sighing will flee away."

Psalm 23
Revelation 3:20
Matthew 13:24-30
Revelation 21:22-27
Revelation 22:1-5

Yesterday's Gone

Yesterday is gone, but tomorrow is fast approaching
Don't allow its worries to be intruding and encroaching
Like cancer's little fingers, worry spreads and then brings death
Affecting mind and spirit, and eventually your breath

Live each day with faith and know I will provide
Seek My will in prayer, let My Spirit be your guide
Yes, there will be troubles, eternity will prove their worth
If you see with My eyes, its treasures you'll unearth

The mountaintop is great, but you can't stay there long
It's in the lush, fertile valley, your faith will prove it's strong
Mountain streams will pour down, to refresh and give you hope
Take time to rest and meet with Me, on its grassy, gentle slope

Do not dwell on yesterday, it's gone and can't be changed
Surrender all to Me, so peace can be exchanged
You can't run a race looking backward—it causes you to fall
Look toward the finish line, and hear reward's loud call

April 20, 2019

Romans 8:28—"And we know that in all things God works for the good of those who love him, who have been called according to his purpose."

Psalm 23
Romans 8:28-39
Acts 20:22-24
1 Corinthians 9:24-27
2 Timothy 4:6-18

Me in You

Me in you and you in Me
That is how it's meant to be
A love that is full I will impart
To satisfy every waiting heart

Then take this love and give it away
Since you didn't earn it, you can't repay
The combined worth of the stars and sun
Cannot equal the value of each saved one

This union is a mystery so deep
My love for you does not slumber, sleep
Its passion always burning bright
Even in the darkest night

I am the Word you must obey
I am the Way you must go each day
My Truth is revealed to all who search
My Life is found in My bride, the church

Together, forever, we will reign on high
My queen, My love, the apple of My eye
For you did forsake all to become My wife
Your choice was the Way, the Truth, and the Life

August 17, 2018

John 14:20-23—"On that day you will realize that I am in my Father, and you are in me, and I am in you. [21] Whoever has my commands and keeps them is the one who loves

me. The one who loves me will be loved by my Father, and I too will love them and show myself to them."
²² Then Judas (not Judas Iscariot) said, "But, Lord, why do you intend to show yourself to us and not to the world?"

²³ Jesus replied, "Anyone who loves me will obey my teaching. My Father will love them, and we will come to them and make our home with them."

John 14
Psalm 121:3-4

Drifting Away

Oh, anchor of my soul, don't let me drift away
The cares and pleasures of this life can cause my heart to stray
Swift and strong are currents deep, propelling me along
Before I know, I'm far away, from where I do belong

Rescue me with searching beam from Your lighthouse on the hill
Illuminate the rocky reefs, which lie in wait to kill
Let Your light cut through the fog, in the storm's strong surge
I reach to grab its luminous ray and from the gale emerge

Bring me safe into Your harbor, never more to stray
In You is life, eternal truth, and the only way
Greater love has no one, than He saves His friend from death
I will praise You all my life, even till final breath

When I cross over Jordan's river to the other side
Let this be my song, my story—in You I abide
Never more to drift away, Your likeness I'll reflect
To join with other spirits of righteous men made perfect

May 26, 2018

Hebrews 2:1-3—"We must pay the most careful attention, therefore, to what we have heard, *so that we do not drift away*. ² For since the message spoken through angels was binding, and every violation and disobedience received its just punishment, ³ how shall we escape if we ignore so great a salvation? This salvation, which was first announced by the Lord, was confirmed to us by those who heard him."

Hebrews 6:19-20—"We have this hope as an anchor for the soul, firm and secure. It enters the inner sanctuary behind the curtain, [20] where our forerunner, Jesus, has entered on our behalf. He has become a high priest forever, in the order of Melchizedek."

Acts 27:13-44
Hebrews 2:10-18
Hebrews 12:22-25
John 14:15-21

Remain in Me

Remain in Me, and I will remain in you
I am the true vine, with majesty endued
I've watered, fed and pruned thee, in My vineyard fair
I delight in your harvest, producing fragrance in the air

This is for My Father's glory, that you bear much fruit
You did not choose Me, you were My pursuit
You once were My servant, but now I call you friend
If you remain in Me, faithful until the end

As the Father loves Me, so I now love you
You will remain in Me, if My commandments you pursue
Share what I have given you and love each other well
Greater love has no one than He saves His friend from hell

You are My friend if you do what I command
This is not an option you need to understand
If you do not remain in Me, your situation's dire
Such branches are picked up and thrown into the fire

I am the true vine, My Father is the gardener
He cuts off every fruitless branch to display My splendor
If you remain in Me, ask Me what you will
It's for My Father's glory, His purpose to fulfill

March 15, 2018

John 15:5-8—"I am the vine; you are the branches. If you remain in me and I in you, you will bear much fruit; apart from me you can do nothing. ⁶ If you do not remain in me, you are like a branch that is thrown away and withers; such branches are picked up, thrown into the fire and burned.⁷ If you remain in me and my words remain in you, ask whatever you wish, and it will be done for you. ⁸ This is to my Father's glory, that you bear much fruit, showing yourselves to be my disciples."

James 5:19-20—"My brothers and sisters, if one of you should wander from the truth and someone should bring that person back, ²⁰ remember this: whoever turns a sinner from the error of their way will save them from death and cover over a multitude of sins."

John 15:1-17
Hebrews 10:26-39
Revelation 2:4-7
Revelation 3:1-5

Counted Worthy

God's righteous judgment is impartial, perfect and true
He will pay back trouble, to those who trouble you
This will happen when Jesus is revealed in blazing fire
For sinners and unbelievers, their situation is very dire

But for those who love God— those saints who overcome
Will be counted worthy, to receive a glorious welcome
Ancient gates will swing wide, a rapturous sight to behold
With unspeakable glories to experience, never before seen or told

To be counted worthy, means suffering for Jesus' sake
Valuing the eternal while worldly things forsake
Immeasurable treasure attaining—more desirable than gold
Can be found in the Bible—precious promises of old

April 24, 2019

2 Thessalonians 1:5—"All this is evidence that God's judgment is right, and as a result you will be counted worthy of the kingdom of God, for which you are suffering."

2 Thessalonians 1:5-12
2 Corinthians 12:2-4
Revelation 21

Live in Obedience

Though you see no eye, I am watching you
Though you seek no voice, I am calling anew
Yours is the freedom to choose a good or bad way
Will you walk your own path or choose to obey?

My grace is abundant, My mercy so deep
Indifference grieves My Spirit, in intercession I weep
Your search for holiness arrives at no easy road
It's the result of those, who make Me their abode

To live in obedience is to walk in My power
In the day of calamity, I will be your high tower
Nothing can harm you except it first passes Me
Trials and temptations prove loves fervency

Inscribe My words on the doorposts of your heart
There they will dwell and their wisdom impart
Then you will win favor and a good name
Let this be your testimony, "I overcame"

September 27, 2018

Proverbs 3:3-4—"Let love and faithfulness never leave you; bind them around your neck, write them on the tablet of your heart. ⁴Then you will win favor and a good name in the sight of God and man."

Deuteronomy 6:4-9—"Hear, O Israel: The Lord our God, the Lord is one. ⁵You shall love the Lord your God with all your heart and with all your soul and with all your might. ⁶And these words that I command you today shall be on your heart. ⁷ You shall teach them diligently to your children, and shall talk of them when you sit in your house, and when you walk by the way, and when you lie down, and when you rise. ⁸ You shall bind them as a sign on your hand, and they shall be as frontlets between your eyes.⁹ You shall write them on the doorposts of your house and on your gates."

Proverbs 1 & 2
Hebrews 10:32-39
Revelation 12:10-11

A Priceless Treasure

Dance, dance with all of your might
Rejoice in the Lord, celebrate in His sight
Raise your arms and give praise to Him
Let overflowing joy fill your heart to the brim

The earth is the Lord's and the fullness thereof
Also the sky and the stars up above
They move like clockwork to an orchestrated plan
To the beat of God's heart toward His creation——man

One by one He forms us into His likeness with care
All with talents and features so rare
The worth of each person is a priceless treasure
Filled with God's breath and love without measure

"Valuable, so valuable, you are to Me"
Says the One who reigns eternally
Grace without measure, mercy so wide
Provided to those who in Him do abide

December 9, 2017

2 Samuel 6:14-15—"Wearing a linen ephod, David was dancing before the Lord with all his might, [15] while he and all Israel were bringing up the ark of the Lord with shouts and the sound of trumpets."

2 Samuel 6:14-23
Psalm 149
Psalm 24
Psalm 139:13-18
Genesis 2:4-7
Psalm 80:1

CHAPTER 6

Great Grace

Incense Altar—Great Grace

The last article of furniture in the Holy Place was the incense altar made of gold. Every morning and evening, incense was to be burned. You need fire to start incense—a picture of God's power. As prayer and intercession went forth, God released angelic forces upon those with a pure heart who were calling out to Him. Our prayers mingle with the will of God to bring His will to earth. As the smoke rose, it was a picture of our prayers rising to heaven. It was a time to call upon God and He would answer with His mercy and Great Grace.

Great Grace

Grace, grace, grace, is what I breathe on you
See it drifts down gently, as the morning dew
Settling on your path, even before you venture out
Call on Me in faith, believe and do not doubt

I'm searching for those hearts who surrender to My will
To carry out My plans, My desires to fulfill
This may look like nothing you will be expecting
For it might include—rejecting and disrespecting

My unmerited favor, I pour out on you
Along with faith and love, these you must pursue
They are found in Me, there is no other way
Ask and you'll receive, My grace for each new day

Impart this grace to others, by prayer, in faith and love
I will surely answer from My throne room up above
Then the world will see and know the love of My dear Son
My great grace, has great power, to transform everyone

May 31, 2019

2 Corinthian's 12:9-10—"But he said to me, "My grace is sufficient for you, for my power is made perfect in weakness." Therefore, I will boast all the more gladly about my weaknesses, so that Christ's power may rest on me. [10] That is why, for Christ's sake, I delight in weaknesses, in insults, in hardships, in persecutions, in difficulties. For when I am weak, then I am strong."

1 Timothy 1:14—"The grace of our Lord was poured out on me abundantly, along with the faith and love that are in Christ Jesus."

Ephesians 2:1-10
Ephesians 3:1-13
2 Timothy 1:9-12
Hebrews 4:16

A Pure Heart

Help me to love You with a heart that is pure
For only by Your promises can I hope to endure
My flesh is weak, so easily I stray
Off life's path, marked "narrow way"

Call on Me out of a pure heart
I will hear from on high and My Word impart
Who may ascend the hill of the Lord?
Those who love Me and obey My Word

Whatever is true, pure, noble and right
Think on those things, precious in My sight
Then My peace will alight upon you
Guarding your heart and mind with Morning Star's dew

December 25, 2017

Matthew 5:8—"Blessed are the pure in heart, for they shall see God."

Psalm 24:3-4a—"Who may ascend into the hill of the Lord? And who may stand in His holy place? [4] He who has clean hands and a pure heart…"

Proverbs 15:26
Philippians 4:8-9
2 Timothy 2:22-26
Titus 1:15-16
Song of Solomon 5:2

Morning's Prayer

Waiting, listening, praying—with a humble heart
Greeting You each morning, is how I like to start
In my soul's sweet silence, a whisper in my ear
Thoughts and pictures in my mind let me know You're near

As my eyes read through Your Book, my heart is touched by fire
Glory shines from each page, to ponder and inspire
Sacred Words, sent from heaven, implanted in my heart
Power to love, to live and die, the Spirit does impart

Looking out the window, of my searching soul
I see You in each person, circumstance and goal
Each life has a purpose You've gifted them to bear
Each soul a treasure with qualities so rare

Give me wisdom, grace and love, to face the coming day
Help me find the narrow path that leads to heaven's way
Each encounter, every thought, recorded for all time
Living my life for Your glory, a story so sublime

February 5, 2019

Psalm 5:3—"In the morning, LORD, you hear my voice; in the morning I lay my requests before you and wait expectantly."

Malachi 3:16-18
Daniel 7:9-10
Luke 10:20

God's Voice

Call upon Me for I am Faithful and True
My words drop unannounced like morning dew
They glisten like diamonds reflecting the light
Imparting direction, truth, wisdom and sight

Wait in My Presence, expectant to hear
Words that will edify, bring hope and cheer
I am with you always, even to the end
You are My beloved, My bride, My friend

Listen for the answer to your hearts cry
As angels are dispatched with My reply
Others hear only thunder, but My beloved ones know
The voice of their Savior in the earth below

September 1, 2017

John 12:28-29—"Father, glorify your name!"

"Then a voice came from heaven, "I have glorified it, and will glorify it again." ²⁹ The crowd that was there and heard it said it had thundered; others said an angel had spoken to him."

John 10:2-4—"The one who enters by the gate is the shepherd of the sheep.³ The gatekeeper opens the gate for him, and the sheep listen to his voice. He calls his own sheep by name and leads them out. ⁴ When he has brought out all his own, he goes on ahead of them, and his sheep follow him because they know his voice."

Revelation 19:11
Isaiah 30:20-21
Psalm 91:9-12
Hebrews 1:14

    The ones who draw close to God, seeking Him, are the ones who will hear His voice clearly. When a voice came from heaven from the Father, answering Jesus, the disciple who wrote the gospel John clearly heard what was said by God and recorded it. But some there only heard thunder; others thought an angel spoke. There were three different opinions to the source of the voice and what the sound was.
    Ones not concerned with spiritual things heard only thunder. Others knew the sound came from the heavenly realm, but they couldn't hear the message. But John, the beloved disciple, heard clearly.

Unseen forces

Angels standing guard are watching over me
Sent from Father's throne to those on bended knee
They might be there to comfort, or catch a falling tear
Though we cannot see them, they are always near

Angels rejoice when we are faithful to the Lord above
They join us in praising God with hearts full of love
Their heavenly music fills the air, but does not reach our ear
Resplendent glory emanates to charge the atmosphere

Prayers to God direct these unseen forces to move on His behalf
These angels form a powerful army to consummate Gods wrath
A mighty battle cry goes forth—angelic forces charge
Sent to take contested ground—God's kingdom to enlarge

The Father sends a message, winged messengers take flight
A whisper in our ear, reflects a new insight
He makes His angels spirits, His servant's flames of fire
Sent to do His will, fulfilling His desires

Heavenly portals open, swift messengers come down
Earthly tasks completed, without alarm or sound
Reflecting God's great glory, they serve both God and man
They delight to do His will and fulfill His every plan

December 30, 2018

Hebrews 1:7—"In speaking of the angels he says, "He makes his angels spirits, and his servant's flames of fire."

Hebrews 1
Psalm 103:20-21
Psalm 91:9-12
Genesis 28:10-15

Overcoming Power

Help me to be obedient and walk in Your ways
You alone are worthy of all of my praise
Only the pure in heart will see Your face
Impart to me now—Your mercy, love, and grace

With Your praise in my mouth and Your sword in my hand
Prepare me to do battle against the evil in my land
I praise You with dancing, let music rise in the night
As You fill Your people with Your glory and Your might

Princes of darkness are bound by the power of Your Word
The sentence written against them is delivered and heard
This is the glory, all Your saints will come to know
As Your Spirit is poured out and revival fires glow

Praise God in His sanctuary—the place He does dwell
Praise Him with instruments, His glory foretell
Oh, praise the Lord, everyone who has breath
He has delivered us from evil and the power of death

June 26, 2019

Psalm 149:6-9—"May the praise of God be in their mouths and a double-edged sword in their hands, [7] to inflict vengeance on the nations and punishment on the peoples, [8] to bind their kings with fetters, their nobles with shackles of iron, [9] to carry out the sentence written against them —this is the glory of all his faithful people. Praise the LORD."

Ephesians 6:17—"Take the helmet of salvation and the sword of the Spirit, which is the word of God."

Psalm 149
Psalm 150

Holy Spirit Power

Listen to the wind as it travels through the night
It is like My Spirit, hidden from men's sight
This wind can be felt and detected by the ear
But none knows where it comes from, or where it will appear

Follow in My footsteps, though they can't be seen
If you listen closely, My direction you will glean
It is not by power or might, but by My Spirit, says the Lord
You can clearly know My will, when all are in accord

On the day of Pentecost, My Spirit came with power
Unity and love were present, in those gathered at that hour
That is the secret, to those waiting for My might
To those whose thoughts are pure—and in My ways delight

My prayer is not for them alone, but to all who will believe
So that the world will know I love them, My glory they'll receive
I am in them and you in Me, so we may be as one
In unity and love we'll dwell, in My Kingdom under the Son

April 15, 2019

John 3:5-8—"Jesus answered, "Very truly I tell you, no one can enter the kingdom of God unless they are born of water and the Spirit. [6] Flesh gives birth to flesh, but the Spirit gives birth to spirit. [7] You should not be surprised at my saying, 'You must be born again.' [8] The wind blows wherever it pleases. You hear its sound, but you cannot tell where it comes from or where it is going. So it is with everyone born of the Spirit."

Zechariah 4:6—"So he said to me, "This is the word of the LORD to Zerubbabel: 'Not by might nor by power, but by my Spirit,' says the LORD Almighty."

Acts 2
John 17

    I arose at 2:22 AM, feeling wide-awake. As I sat down to listen to what the Lord might be speaking to me, I heard the wind blowing loudly outside my bedroom window. Is this what the Lord was showing me? I waited some more and this poem came into my mind.

Follow Close Behind

Me:
I commit to You my hopes and my fears
Even everyone and everything I hold most dear
You are calling me to live and walk by faith alone
Help me break old patterns to which I am prone

Lord:
The time is now because the hour is late
The day of My return is a fast approaching date
Follow close behind Me as you run the lifelong race
In sight is the finish line where we'll meet face-to-face

Be alert and keep your thoughts always on Me
Distractions will be many, but I am your victory
When faith and love reach up, My power will descend
My angels go with you to help protect and defend

March 14, 2019

Proverbs 3:5-6—"Trust in the LORD with all your heart and lean not on your own understanding;
⁶ in all your ways submit to him, and he will make your paths straight."

Proverbs 2

"Obedience in the fear of God is the beginning of wisdom, but the fullness of wisdom is to obey because of your love for God. Then you will see the power and the glory." From, "The Call," by Rick Joyner, page 61.

Vineyard of the Lord

My heart is deceitful, it can even deceive me
I want to walk in His ways and be clothed with humility
My loud sinful nature demands its own way
Lord, help me to walk in truth, and die to self every day

The Lord prunes His vineyard to be even more fruitful and strong
He waters and lovingly tends those, who to Him do belong
As He checks on His harvest, He cuts off the diseased parts
So they do not infect the branches of those with pure hearts

Do not despise the Lord's discipline and ignore your pain
It produces a harvest for those who have been trained
With a glad heart submit to His correction and love
Fix your eyes on Jesus, the true vine from above

January 25, 2019

Hebrews 12:2-6—"Let us fix our eyes on Jesus, the author and perfecter of our faith, who for the joy set before him endured the cross, scorning its shame, and sat down at the right hand of the throne of God. ³ Consider him who endured such opposition from sinful men, so that you will not grow weary and lose heart."

⁴ In your struggle against sin, you have not yet resisted to the point of shedding your blood. ⁵ And you have forgotten that word of encouragement that addresses you as sons:

"My son, do not make light of the Lord's discipline, and do not lose heart when he rebukes you, ⁶ because the Lord disciplines those he loves, and he punishes everyone he accepts as a son."

Jeremiah 17:9-10 (NKJV)—"The heart *is* deceitful above all *things,* and desperately wicked;
Who can know it? [10] I, the Lord, search the heart; I test the mind, even to give every man according to his ways, according to the fruit of his doings."

John 15:1-17
1 Corinthians 5
Hebrews 12:1-13

David's Pursuit

As David penned his psalms of praise
Worship from his heart would raise
Doubt would flee and faith would win
God's voice he'd hear from deep within

Mysteries revealed and visions shown
Of future things that were not known
All of these did God impart
To David's humble waiting heart

A prince among men, God's close friend
Brought forth a dynasty that will never end
Throughout the years his words proved true
God's heart was what David did pursue

September 5, 2017

Acts 13:22—"After removing Saul, he made David their king. God testified concerning him: 'I have found David son of Jesse, a man after my own heart; he will do everything I want him to do.'"

Psalm 138
Psalm 22

CHAPTER 7

Go Beyond the Veil

The Curtain or Veil—Go Beyond the Veil

The veil separated the Holy Place from the Holy of Holies. No one could go past it—except for the High Priest once a year on the Day of Atonement, so he could sprinkle blood on the mercy seat to atone for the nation of Israel's sin. Now, because Jesus died for our sins, the veil was torn in two pieces. It no longer separates the two rooms. We now have access to the mercy seat in the Holy of Holies, so feel free to—Go Beyond the Veil.

Go Beyond the Veil

I'm desperate to hear a living word from You
Let Your Presence fall on me like morning dew
I can't see You coming, but refreshment does await
To those laying at Your feet remaining prostrate

Outside the rain falls, but inside a drought
Not sensing Your Presence brings on many a fear and doubt
The skies are as brass; I can't hear or see a thing
Till I go beyond the veil and approach my Lord and King

In faith I see You now, waiting patiently for me
You were there all along, I just couldn't see
Earthly things had dimmed my eyes and my heart
I couldn't see or hear what You wanted to impart

Sometimes we are content to live in the outer court
Sometimes we go to others for comfort and support
Go through the Holy Place, His Presence to avail
The Holy Spirit beckons us to go beyond the veil

February 24, 2018

Hebrews 10:19-22—"Therefore, brothers and sisters, since we have confidence to enter the Most Holy Place by the blood of Jesus, [20] by a new and living way opened for us through the curtain (veil), that is, his body, [21] and since we have a great priest over the house of God, [22] let us draw near to God."

Psalm 5
Psalm 11:4-5
Psalm 15

Matthew 27:50-54
Hebrews 9:1-14
Hebrews 10:19-24

    A period of worry had settled over my mind and heart. I hadn't received a word or poem from the Lord for a long period of time. So, I spent time waiting to hear and this poem came to me. This poem was my prayer.

Come Through the Holy Place

Me:
I come to the Holy Place to partake of its delights
Experiencing the wonder as the Holy Spirit alights
Lord, come and lead me by Your hand through this exalted place
As I wait to hear Your words, and see You face to face

Light Your holy lampstand, so I can see the way
The beauty of Your Presence shines from its glorious ray
This light exposes my dark places, hidden deep in me
Help me step into Your glory and from my sin be free

Lord:
I invite you to the table where fresh bread is for the taking
I am the "Bread from Heaven," to be gathered upon awakening
Eat your fill of My fresh Word I daily send to you
Find strength and guidance in this meal as your spirit is renewed

Come with incense to the altar looking for My fire
As the offering is lit, your prayers ascend much higher
This fire will burn and purify till the dross is all withdrawn
As this pleasing fragrance comes to Me, know I will respond

Come into My Presence, the curtain has been torn
A way was made to enter here because of Easter morn
Linger in My Presence; share your day with Me
You must come through the Holy Place, to gain eternity

April 7, 2018

Psalm 65:4—"Blessed are those you choose and bring near to live in your courts! We are filled with the good things of your house, of your holy temple."

Hebrews 12:14—"Make every effort to live in peace with everyone and to be holy; without holiness no one will see the Lord."

Exodus 33:9-11
1 John 1:5-10
Exodus 16:10-35
Malachi 3:1-4
Hebrews 9 and 10

Pursuing God's Presence

"Don't let me fail You," I pray each day
On the side roads of life, it's easy to drift away
The pleasures of life can lull me to sleep
While cares of this life tend to pull me so deep

I tend to forget You are always with me
You hear everything and Your watchful eyes see
How different would I live if I could see You?
Open my eyes as Your Presence I pursue

You speak to me through those I would not choose
If I don't humble myself, Your message I could lose
You stand afar off from the self-righteous and proud
I draw close to You with a heart that is bowed

I invite You to come and share each day with me
Reveal to me things I normally wouldn't see
I ask You, Lord, for wisdom, mercy and grace
To help win the crown at the end of the race

June 27, 2017

2 Timothy 4:6-8—"For I am already being poured out like a drink offering, and the time for my departure is near. [7] I have fought the good fight, I have finished the race, I have kept the faith. [8] Now there is in store for me the crown of righteousness, which the Lord, the righteous Judge, will award to me on that day—and not only to me, but also to all who have longed for his appearing."

Micah 6:8—"He has shown you, O mortal, what is good. And what does the Lord require of you? To act justly and to love mercy and to walk humbly with your God."

Romans 13:11-14
1 Thessalonians 5:1-10
Psalm 89:15-17
1 Peter 5:5-6
Revelation 3:20

With Unveiled Faces

Who may ascend the mountain of the Lord?
Those with pure hearts who tremble at His Word
The King resides there, with His glory on display
Shining brighter than the sun in the middle of the day

Moses saw this glory as he met with the Most High
It caused his face to shine creating fear in those nearby
He had asked to see God's glory, now it reflects off him
A veil was needed on his face until the glory dimmed

This same veil still covers eyes of those upon the earth
Until they turn to Jesus and experience a "new birth"
Then with unveiled faces, look into His glory
Being transformed into His likeness now is mandatory

Lift up your gates, oh my heart, open up the door
So the King of Glory may come in, my motives to explore
Let me gaze upon Your glory exposing my dark places
Send Your glory now to shine, on those with unveiled faces

March 12, 2018

Psalm 43:3—"Send me your light and your faithful care, let them lead me; let them bring me to your holy mountain, to the place where you dwell."

2 Corinthians 3:15-18—"Even to this day when Moses is read, a veil covers their hearts. [16] But whenever anyone turns to the Lord, the veil is taken away. [17] Now the Lord is the Spirit, and where the Spirit of the Lord is, there is freedom. [18] And we all, who with unveiled faces contemplate the Lord's glory, are

being transformed into his image with ever-increasing glory, which comes from the Lord, who is the Spirit."

Psalm 24
Exodus 33
Exodus 34
2 Corinthians 3:7-18
John 3:1-21

Prepare the Way

Prepare; prepare, the way for the Lord
The voice in the desert cannot be ignored
Repent; repent, for the day is at hand
Wisdom calls out throughout all the land

A shaking is sifting out hearts that are pure
In the day of His coming, who can endure?
A refining fire is separating dross
From those who are willing to take up His cross

Prepare; prepare, for the day draws near
When the Son of God in the skies will appear
Robed in splendor He will come amongst the clouds
With the armies of heaven shouting praises aloud

Repent; repent, for the day draws near
When the glory of heaven will rend the atmosphere
Will you be ready and watching when He comes?
When the heavens are opened for the millenniums

July 31, 2017

Mark 1:1-4—"The beginning of the good news about Jesus the Messiah, the Son of God, [2] as it is written in Isaiah the prophet:

"I will send my messenger ahead of you, who will prepare your way" [3] "a voice of one calling in the wilderness, 'Prepare the way for the Lord, make straight paths for him.' [4] And so

John the Baptist appeared in the wilderness, preaching a baptism of repentance for the forgiveness of sins."

Malachi 3:1-5
Acts 1:9-11
Isaiah 40:1-5
Revelation 19:11-14
Matthew 24:42-44
Revelation 20:1-6

My Eternal Home

My eternal home is being prepared lovingly for me
With my deepest desires and wishes it will be built accordingly
But best of all, I'll see dear faces who have gone on before
They will be there to welcome me when I step inside the door

Earthly shadows fading, in the light of heaven's bliss
The pain and struggles left behind I surely will not miss
We will know, as we are known, with perfect love and grace
Eternal youth and beauty will shine from every face

Heavenly music will fill the air, praising the Lord on high
Angels attending to God's work, we'll see as they go by
Creativity, loosed inside each person, will fulfill their destiny
Perfect unity, love and peace is the atmosphere eternally

My eternal home cannot be found on this present earth
All of the world's riches could not equal its true heavenly worth
Treasures God's Word promises, I am working to acquire
Rewards that will be left, after passing through God's fire

April 26, 2019

1 Timothy 6:18-19—"Command them to do good, to be rich in good deeds, and to be generous and willing to share. *19* In this way they will lay up treasure for themselves as a firm foundation for the coming age, so that they may take hold of the life that is truly life."

1 Corinthians 3:13-15—"Their work will be shown for what it is, because the Day will bring it to light. It will be revealed

with fire, and the fire will test the quality of each person's work. ¹⁴ If what has been built survives, the builder will receive a reward. ¹⁵ If it is burned up, the builder will suffer loss but yet will be saved—even though only as one escaping through the flames."

John 14
Revelation 21, 22

My Father's House

My Father's house is being built
With living stones of dust and silt
The foundation is Jesus, the Cornerstone
Who took on flesh departing heaven's throne

These living stones form a temple high
Where God's Spirit descends to occupy
Spiritual sacrifices are offered there
Acceptable to God because of Christ's despair

This Stone is precious to those who believe
Eternal life is what they receive
This same Stone causes others to fall
Because they disobey the message—their pitfall

These chosen people belonging to God
Declare His praises as they walk earth's sod
They have been called out of darkness into wonderful light
To rescue others from sin and give them new sight

My Father's house is large and wide
An invitation is extended to come in and abide
Grace and mercy are there, with room for all
A feast is waiting in God's banquet hall

October 9, 2017

Revelation 22:17—"The Spirit and the bride say, "Come!" And let the one who hears say, "Come!" Let the one who is thirsty come; and let the one who wishes take the free gift of the water of life."

1 Peter 2:4-10
1 Corinthians 3:9-15
Ephesians 2:19-22
Mark 15:34
Acts 26:17-18
John 14

I Am Waiting

Ask of me; I will show you many things
Listen to the message My Holy Spirit brings
In quietness and rest, you'll hear a still, small voice
Each day you must surrender, each day you have a choice

I am nearer than you think, closer than you know
There is much I want to tell you, much I want to show
Know that I am waiting, please come and speak with Me
I love when you ask Me questions with heartfelt honesty

Know it is My joy, to come and speak with you
Patiently I wait, as worldly pleasures you pursue
Come aside and join Me, at our secret place
Sweet friendship is waiting, as we meet face-to-face

Yes, Lord, I will follow You with all of my heart
I will meet You at our secret place, and set some time apart
Show me what I need to ask, what I need to know
Be my wisdom and my council in the Spirit's flow

November 3, 2018

Song of Songs 2:14—"My dove in the clefts of the rock, in the hiding places on the mountainside, show me your face, let me hear your voice; for your voice is sweet, and your face is lovely."

Isaiah 30:21
Isaiah 48:5-8
Jeremiah 33:2-3
Matthew 6:6

Watchman on the Wall

"Watchman, watchman, on the wall, tell Me what you see"
"Shadowy figures in the night, moving stealthily"
"Watchman, watchman, on the wall, sound out the alarm
If no sound is given, the enemies' plans will do much harm"

"A little lamb from Master's flock, I see turning from the way"
"Watchman, watchman, on the wall, bid him now to stay
Tell him of My plans for him, tell him of My love
Let him know I see his heart, from My throne above"

"Now I see a fire prepared, for those who die in sin
Turn back, turn back, I called in vain, above the clamoring din"
"Watchman, watchman, on the wall, you have saved yourself
If you had not warned them, I would have dealt with you Myself"

"Watchman, watchman, on the wall, tell them what you see
If they heed unto your voice, there'll be no catastrophe
Call them to do what's right and just, and they will surely live
All their past transgressions, I will then forgive"

"Forgive me, Lord, for keeping silent, when I ought to speak
Let me clearly hear Your words, that gives strength to the weak
Give me courage to the task and answer when You call
Yes, Lord, I will obey and be Your watchman on the wall"

May 6, 2019

Ezekiel 33:7-9—"Son of man, I have made you a watchman for the people of Israel; so hear the word I speak and give them warning from me. **⁸** When I say to the wicked, 'You wicked person, you will surely die,' and you do not speak out to dissuade them from their ways, that wicked person will die for their sin, and I will hold you accountable for their blood. **⁹** But if you do warn the wicked person to turn from their ways and they do not do so, they will die for their sin, though you yourself will be saved."

Ezekiel 3:16-27
Ezekiel 33:1-20
Ezekiel 18
Habakkuk 2:1-3

    In ancient Israel, watchmen were stationed on the walls and gates of the city to warn of impending attacks or announce approaching messengers.
    Prophets and priests were considered spiritual watchmen as they relayed God's word to the people. From the very beginning God put Adam in the garden and told him to take care of it—or watch over it. Are not all believers called to be watchmen even though each of us has different spheres of responsibility?
    All Christians are called to hear God's voice and follow Him. (John 10). We are to be watching for His coming and know the signs of the times. If we are following His Spirit, we will be obedient to do what we hear Him say.

Worthy is the Lamb

Worthy, worthy is the Lamb, slain on my behalf
A sacrifice that was prepared from eon's dim dark past
God's own Son was sent to die, standing in my place
Stripped of His celestial garments, choosing death's disgrace

Beautiful, so beautiful, are His feet that walked
Into dusty towns of foes, who cruelly jeered and mocked
His loving arms reached out to touch, the lost, the sick, the blind
Showing through His sinless life, God's love to all mankind

This same Jesus bore our sins upon a cursed tree
He took our place and paid the price, so we could be set free
Placed within a brand new tomb, He entered Sheol's domain
Snatching keys from death's cold fingers in Hell's sub terrain

Rising from the grave, Jesus ascended high
Leading captives in His train to His home up in the sky
Now, His blood in Heaven's Temple, redeems all who believe
Heavens mercy and forgiveness is what they receive

"Worthy are You, Lord and God, to receive all glory,"
That is what we will be saying, as each recount their story
"Worthy, worthy is the Lamb"—Proclaim it now with me
Glory, praise, and honor to Jesus, King of Majesty

September 29, 2018

Philippians 2:5-11—"In your relationships with one another, have the same mindset as Christ Jesus: **6** Who, being in very nature God, did not consider equality with God something to be used to his own advantage; ⁷ rather, he made himself nothing by taking the very nature of a servant, being made in human likeness. ⁸ And being found in appearance as a man, he humbled himself by becoming obedient to death— even death on a cross! ⁹ Therefore God exalted him to the highest place and gave him the name that is above every name, ¹⁰ that at the name of Jesus every knee should bow, in heaven and on earth and under the earth, ¹¹ and every tongue acknowledge that Jesus Christ is Lord, to the glory of God the Father.

Ephesians 1:4-10, 4:8-10
Revelation 1:18; 9:1; 20:1
Hebrews 9
Revelation 4:9-11

The Riches of His Glory

Which of us can see or know the riches of God's glory?
Eternity's not long enough to discover its inventory
No worlds created can contain its manifested weight
Unknown dimensions traveled to reveal its vast estate

But yet, He longs to share with us the riches of His glory
Because we shared His sufferings along life's journeys' story
Heirs of God, co-heirs with Christ, of glories vast estate
There is no way to measure it, appraise or calculate

Our present sufferings can't compare to this eternal glory
These momentary troubles are fleeting and transitory
Heavenly glory—revealed in us—to all who do await
The coming of our God and King, forever to celebrate

December 7, 2017

Romans 9:23—"What if he did this to make the riches of his glory known to the objects of his mercy, whom he prepared in advance for glory."

Romans 8:17-18—"Now if we are children, then we are heirs—heirs of God and co-heirs with Christ, if indeed we share in his sufferings in order that we may also share in his glory. [18] I consider that our present sufferings are not worth comparing with the glory that will be revealed in us."

Ephesians 2:6-7
Ephesians 3:8-21

Romans 9:23-26
2 Corinthians 4:16-18
1 Peter 4:12-16
1 Peter 5:1

For Those Who Overcome

Let Me hear your gentle voice telling Me of your love
My longing heart waits to hear in anticipation from above
Your yearning hope calls out in faith to touch the Father's heart
As I hear each prayer that rises—grace and mercy I impart

Know I am behind the scene to work all things for your good
You'd thank Me for each fiery trial, if you understood
Each pruned branch produces fruit in the Father's vineyard
A praising heart that sings through trials is a pleasing spikenard

If you knew what reward awaits, for those who overcome
You'd die to self, choose the cross, and welcome martyrdom
No good deed will go unnoticed in the Father's ledger
Hearing, "Well done," on that great "day" will be the greatest treasure

December 16, 2018

2 Corinthians 4:16-18—"Therefore we do not lose heart. Though outwardly we are wasting away, yet inwardly we are being renewed day by day. *17* For our light and momentary troubles are achieving for us an eternal glory that far outweighs them all. *18* So we fix our eyes not on what is seen, but on what is unseen, since what is seen is temporary, but what is unseen is eternal."

2 Corinthians 4
Romans 8:23-39
Matthew 25:21

Spikenard is a sweet-smelling ointment used by the ancients. It is produced by crushing flowers and then mixing it with oil. It is a picture of us going through trials and being crushed—but in the bruising, exuding a sweet nature and coming out of our experience with a praising faith-filled attitude.

Deep into Gods Heart

Me:
Lord, draw me deep, into the recesses of Your heart
Disclose Your desires, and then Your passion impart
You've been waiting to reveal them, to all who would come
Many are too busy; they find it burdensome

Lord:
Come, take My hand, I have much to share
Hidden passageways and chambers, I will walk with you there
The sound that you hear is the beating of My heart
Lay your head on My chest as My desires I impart

Deep, go down deep, then deeper still
Not many choose the way that leads them downhill
The humble in heart, must bow down to enter there
This secret place can be found, by anyone in prayer

What is hidden in darkness, I will bring to light
Share with Me My sorrows, but also, My delights
Untold mysteries and secrets can be discovered there
The treasures unearthed, are priceless beyond compare

Enoch discovered the way, to this secret place
Nothing was more valuable than meeting with Me, face-to-face
He walked with Me daily, My Presence to pursue
If you follow in his footsteps, one day I will come for you too

June 13, 2019

Deuteronomy 29:29—"The secret things belong to the Lord our God, but the things revealed belong to us and to our children forever, that we may follow all the words of this law."

Matthew 6:5-6—"And when you pray, do not be like the hypocrites, for they love to pray standing in the synagogues and on the street corners to be seen by others. Truly I tell you, they have received their reward in full. **6** But when you pray, go into your room, close the door and pray to your Father, who is unseen. Then your Father, who sees what is done in secret, will reward you."

Mark 4:11—"He told them, "The secret of the kingdom of God has been given to you. But to those on the outside everything is said in parables…"

Matthew 22:1-14
Psalm 139:15-18
1 Corinthians 4:1-5
Hebrews 11:5

CHAPTER 8

Linger in My Presence

The Holy of Holies—Linger in My Presence

The Holy of Holies is where the manifest Presence of God resided in the Temple. The ark of the covenant was in this room all by itself. The lid of it represented the mercy seat of God. The curtain or veil which separated its entrance from the Holy Place was torn in two on the day Jesus died. Those who have placed their trust in Jesus and have come in through the Holy Place are invited to enter by the blood of Jesus. It is there we are invited to—Linger in His Presence.

Linger in My Presence

Come and linger in My Presence, I have much to say
Approach with an attitude of worship, willing to obey
Be mindful you are drawing near, to a Mighty King
I'm sitting on the mercy seat, beneath the cherubim's wings

Come, draw close, in faith and love, the curtain has come down
I want to see you face-to-face, dressed in your righteous gown
How I long to hear your voice and share with Me your thoughts
Listen closely as I speak and from My Word be taught

The worlds were formed at My command and they came into being
Into darkness came My light, I made the eye for seeing
Each one has a choice to make, to know Me and My will
Each life has a destiny, they were created to fulfill

Come into My Presence, in quietness and rest
"Listen for My still small voice," is the King's request
I have much to share with you, My bride, My precious dove
Come and linger in My Presence, you are much beloved

May 7, 2019

Song of Songs 2:14—"My dove in the clefts of the rock, in the hiding places on the mountainside, show me your face, let me hear your voice; for your voice is sweet, and your face is lovely."

Hebrews 10:19-22—"Therefore, brothers and sisters, since we have confidence to enter the Most Holy Place by the blood of Jesus, [20] by a new and living way opened for us through the curtain, that is, his body, [21] and since we have a great priest over the house of God, [22] let us draw near to God with a sincere heart and with the full assurance that faith brings, having our hearts sprinkled to cleanse us from a guilty conscience and having our bodies washed with pure water."

Exodus 25:10-22
Matthew 27:50-51
Revelation 19:7-8

Beauty of Silence

Shush, shush, quiet your soul
Breathe deeply of My Spirit until you are full
In confidence and rest I will minister to you
Lay your head on My shoulder, I will renew

Words are not needed in times like this
In the beauty of silence, devotion and love kiss
With singleness of heart bring Me your praise
Let your mind be at rest as you center your gaze

I have called you apart, to come hear My voice
Taking time to listen, involves a crucial choice
You can be as close to Me, as you desire
In the beauty of silence, My Presence acquire

March 11, 2019

Psalm 46:10—"Be still, and know that I am God; I will be exalted among the nations, I will be exalted in the earth."

Psalm 139:1-18
Psalm 40:1-10

Under Your Wings

Love's swift song is calling strong
My heart to You alone belongs
Night's soft peace allows me rest
Under Your wings, safe in Your nest

I hear Your heartbeat for the lost
My searching eyes behold Your cross
It was love that put You there
Love divine, love so rare

"Into the river of My pleasures come and sink
I am the fountain of life—come rest and drink
There you can wash away your guilt and shame
On the cross I took your sin and blame"

"Like the mighty mountains is My righteousness
It reaches to the clouds with My faithfulness
Come put your trust under the shadow of My wings
Till the long night is past and dawns light sings"

June 3, 2018

Psalm 36:5-9—"Your love, Lord, reaches to the heavens, your faithfulness to the skies. [6] Your righteousness is like the highest mountains, your justice like the great deep. You, Lord, preserve both people and animals. [7] How priceless is your unfailing love, O God! People take refuge in the shadow of your wings. [8] They feast on the abundance of your house; you give them drink from your river of delights. ⁹ For with you is the fountain of life; in your light we see light."

Psalm 17:6-8

Under the Shadow of His Wings

I delight to sit under the shadow of His wings
A place of safety—a place to sing
Those who dwell there, partake of deep rest
Those who are His children—not just a guest

Strength and provision, are provided by God there
Safe under His wings, high up in the air
His faithfulness proves to be your hope and your shield
As you follow His Word and to His ways yield

"Because he loves Me," says the Lord
"I will protect him with My mighty sword
Call upon Me I am mighty to save
From the terror of hell and fear of the grave"

"I will be with him in trouble so grim
With long life I will satisfy him
If you make the Most High your dwelling place
Together forever enjoy excelling grace"

June 26, 2017

Psalm 91:1—"Whoever dwells in the shelter of the Most High will rest in the shadow of the Almighty."

Psalm 91

    There is no place in a nest for a guest. Only the children live there. The verses of Psalm 91 are a promise to those who choose to dwell in the shelter of the Most High under the shadow of His wings.

Walk with Me

My eye is in the center of the swirling pillar of clouds
It roams throughout the earth searching the hearts of the crowds
Dark rain clouds hide My Presence as I ride the ancient sky
Some hear only thunder, but My chosen prophesy

The humble in heart listen to the sound of its meaning
They fall on their knees in intercession, intervening
The brightness of the lightening hides the flashes of angel wings
Grace and mercy are the message their wondrous tiding brings

Do not presume upon this favor that comes from My heart
My saints know the "fear of the Lord" is the place to start
It's the beginning of wisdom and the secret to My power
It must operate in love which in My mercy I do shower

Come, take My hand, I invite you to walk with Me
Make Me your delight in life's long journey
Spacious places and adventures, for you, do wait
As you travel down the road that leads to heaven's gate

October 11, 2018

Genesis 5:24—"Enoch walked faithfully with God…"

2 Chronicles 16:9—"For the eyes of the Lord range throughout the earth to strengthen those whose hearts are fully committed to him…"

Psalm 18
Psalm 68:32-35
2 Chronicles 7:14
Proverbs 9:10
Proverbs 22:4

Prayer Mountain

I'm going to Prayer Mountain, deep into God's heart
The way may be steep and rocky, but I know I've got to start
I'm taking time to listen, to meet the Spirit there
Earthly voices dimming, in the crisp mountain air

I wish that I could see You, and Your form would then appear
Or maybe in the leaves soft rustling, Your gentle voice I'd hear
But then I'd miss that special blessing that others will receive
Because they did not see or hear You, but yet, they did believe

My soul found rest along the way, amongst the fallen trees
Refreshment found its way to me, in a cooling breeze
Softer still, Your peace crept in—fulfilling my desire
In every trilling note of bird, Your praises they'd inspire

Prayer Mountain is a journey to Your waiting heart
Your longing eyes search out for us, hoping soon we'll start
Mountains rise on every side, they bid us come explore
I hear You knocking on my heart, "Please open up the door"

May 6, 2019

Isaiah 56:7—"these I will bring to my holy mountain and give them joy in my house of prayer.
Their burnt offerings and sacrifices will be accepted on my altar; for my house will be called a house of prayer for all nations."

Revelation 3:20—"Here I am! I stand at the door and knock. If anyone hears my voice and opens the door, I will come in and eat with that person, and they with me."

Matthew 6:5-8
Matthew 14:23

I wrote this on Prayer Mountain, in Moravian Falls, North Carolina. People come from all over the world to pray on its lofty peak. Many visitations and visions from the Lord have supposedly taken place on this beautiful, steep mountain. But we really don't have to travel there for God to hear our voice. He hears from His holy mountain any time or place you wish to speak with Him.

You'll Never Walk Alone

You'll never walk alone, for I am by your side
Share your dreams and hopes with Me, and in Me confide
Know I am as close as the hairs upon your head
My generous resources are vast and unlimited

Oh, how I long, to share each day with you
Your hopes, dreams and plans, with Me review
The emptiness inside of you, how I long to fill
Your innermost desires I am working to fulfil

I, the Lord, give you, these desires of your heart
So that you look to Me, to fulfill and to impart
But, make Me your delight, above all these things
Desire Me above all else you hope My hand brings

Learn this secret, then draw close and abide
You'll never be alone, for I am by your side
Let this be your joy and your everlasting song
That you are My beloved, and to God's family belong

December 30, 2017

Psalm 37:4—"Delight yourself in the Lord; and He will give you the desires of your heart."

Psalm 73:23-28
John 14:23
Matthew 28:20
Psalm 20
Psalm 103
Psalm 145

Journey to the Promised Land

You are Mine; you are Mine, the apple of My eye
You are in My thoughts each moment, as I ride the ancient sky
I will be a cloud for you that shields the burning sun—
A fire at night to warm you, when each tiring day is done

I see your every thought as you travel across the sand
I test your every motive in your journey to the Promised Land
Every single need you have I am able to fulfill
Come join Me in My tent, calm your soul, be still

It is in My Presence that you'll find direction for each day
Know I go before you to help prepare the way
I have always been there for you; each need I did attend
Existing outside of time, I am the "Beginning and the End"

At the end of your long journey is the Jordan River
Do not be afraid to enter, I am able to deliver
Never-ending day waits as you leave behind the night—
When you reach the Promised Land, a place of pure delight

February 7, 2019

Deuteronomy 30:15-17—"See, I set before you today life and prosperity, death and destruction.[16] For I command you today to love the Lord your God, to walk in obedience to him, and to keep his commands, decrees and laws; then you will live and increase, and the Lord your God will bless you in the land you are entering to possess.

¹⁷ But if your heart turns away and you are not obedient, and if you are drawn away to bow down to other gods and worship them, **¹⁸** I declare to you this day that you will certainly be destroyed. You will not live long in the land you are crossing the Jordan to enter and possess."

Exodus 33:7—"Now Moses used to take a tent and pitch it outside the camp some distance away, calling it the "tent of meeting." Anyone inquiring of the Lord would go to the tent of meeting outside the camp."

Psalm 68:4, 32, 33
Exodus 33:7-23
Deuteronomy 8:1-3; 10:11-22
Hebrews 11:8-10
Revelation 22:13

How I got this poem:

    I awoke a little after 2 AM and could not sleep, so I got out of bed thinking I could read the Bible until I got sleepy. I asked the Lord where I should read and immediately Psalm 63 came to mind. As I started reading this Psalm, pictures of my day started to come to my mind, and I realized the Lord was close beside me all that day seeing what I was seeing and hearing what I was thinking.
    The first verse…I had just heard a preacher reading this same verse a few hours ago. As I listened to him, my soul thirsted with his to see and hear from the living God. *(¹You, God, are my God, earnestly I seek You; I thirst for You, my whole being longs for You, in a dry and parched land where there is no water.)*

As I read the second, third and fourth verse, I remembered I had thought today about the miracles I had seen with my own eyes in times past and how I long to see them again. *(² I have seen You in the sanctuary and beheld Your power and Your glory. ³ Because Your love is better than life, my lips will glorify You. ⁴ I will praise You as long as I live, and in Your name I will lift up my hands.)*

In the fifth verse, I had just been thinking how much I need to lose weight. The thought came to me that when I get to heaven, I can eat the richest foods and not get fat. *(⁵ I will be fully satisfied as with the richest of foods; with singing lips my mouth will praise You.)*

In the sixth verse, I had just gotten out of bed because I couldn't sleep, so I wanted to read the Bible to hear Gods voice to me. *(⁶ On my bed I remember You; I think of You through the watches of the night.)*

In the seventh and eight verses, just a few hours ago, I had been watching the eagle chicks and other baby birds on the web tucking themselves under their mother's wings. They were so adorable and content, and the mother so attentive. *(⁷ Because You are my help, I sing in the shadow of Your wings. ⁸ I cling to You; Your right hand upholds me.)*

In the ninth and 10th verses, thoughts had come to me during the day of people who don't know the Lord and the eternal destiny of where they are headed. How can I warn them and tell them about how to get to heaven and know the Lord personally? I want them to know the truth so they can escape hell. *(⁹ Those who want to kill me will be destroyed; they will go down to the depths of the earth. ¹⁰ They will be given over to the sword and become food for jackals.)*

As I sat there reading Psalm 63 and marveling at what God was showing to me through this Psalm coinciding with my day's events, a poem came to me, "Journey to the

Promised Land." I finished writing it and went back to bed around 4:30 AM. *(11 But the king will rejoice in God; all who swear by God will glory in Him, while the mouths of liars will be silenced.)*

Abiding in the Secret Place

To obey is better than sacrifice
Trusting My direction should always suffice
Put yourself in My perfect will
The desires of your heart I will fulfill

Oh, My dove, make Me your delight
Sweet is your voice in the dim moonlight
I see you abiding in the secret place
As you linger to meet with Me face-to-face

Arise My darling, My beautiful one
Till the night gives way to everlasting Son
There we will dance on the mountains of spice
Our desires to fulfill and our senses to entice

March 1, 2019

Song of Songs 2:14 (NKJV)—"O my dove, in the clefts of the rock, in the secret places of the cliff, let me see your face, let me hear your voice; for your voice is sweet, and your face is lovely."

1 Samuel 15:22-26
Psalm 37:3-6
Song of Songs 4:1-15
Song of Songs 8:13-14

Run the Race

Consider how the lily grows, in verdant fields so green
Solomon's glory cannot compare to this idyllic scene
The bounty of a thousand acres, are but a minute crop
Of My great riches stored for those, on whom My mercy drops

Heavy rainfall fills the pools, to water all who thirst
My Spirit falls on those who linger, in My Word immersed
Deeper water calls to those who search for treasure rare
Revelation falls on those who wait for Me in prayer

Vast armies wait at My command to rescue those who call
Angels dispatched from My throne, behind the scenes, enthrall
Great clouds of witnesses cheer you on, to conquer in My name
Go forth in faith, subdue in love, My glory to proclaim

Fix your eyes on Me and follow where I lead
Throw off all that hinders and run the race with speed
Great rewards await for those who win an everlasting crown
For those who sacrificed and suffered for Me and My renown

December 24, 2018

1 Corinthian 9:24-25—"Do you not know that in a race all the runners run, but only one gets the prize? Run in such a way as to get the prize. ²⁵ Everyone who competes in the

games goes into strict training. They do it to get a crown that will not last, but we do it to get a crown that will last forever."

Luke 12:22-34
2 Kings 6:8-23
Hebrews 12:1-3
1 Corinthians 9:23-27

Knowledge too Wonderful

Knowledge too wonderful, imagination cannot conceive
The glories of eternity, God's children will receive
Eternal life does not consist of only length of day
It also speaks of quality in wondrous full display

Dimensions not conceived of, colors yet unknown
World's we cannot dream of, is what we will be shown
The past will be forgotten in the midst of all the bliss
Surrounded by His glory, earth's dark shadow we'll not miss

Eternal books will open, truth will then convey
True histories of nations, will be on full display
Heaven's perspective will reveal, God's own loving plan
Written before it happened—the destiny of every man

Knowledge too wonderful, we'll be forever growing
In the love of Christ, faith turns into knowing
But, best of all will be the fact, of His love for me
And that He wants to share His life, with me eternally

April 17, 2019

2 Corinthians 12:2-4—"I know a man in Christ who fourteen years ago was caught up to the third heaven. Whether it was in the body or out of the body I do not know—God knows. ³And I know that this man—whether in the body or apart from the body I do not know, but God knows— ⁴was caught up to paradise and heard inexpressible things, things that no one is permitted to tell."

Psalm 139:6—"Such knowledge is too wonderful for me, too lofty for me to attain."

Romans 16:25-27
Ephesians 1:7-14
Ephesians 2
Ephesians 3:14-21

Wind Song

Lord:
What does the wind say as it whispers through the trees?
How does the owl glide at night as though it clearly sees?
I am always speaking, but many do not hear
I am always present, even very near

The wind of My Spirit can't be seen, but is sometimes heard
My thermals gently lift you like a soaring bird
Come, draw close and hear Me, as I speak to thee
Step forward now in faith, even when you cannot see

Lift your arms to praise Me as the wind begins to blow
Let the music of the night around your branches flow
As My Spirit softly lands upon each waiting heart
Know that council, wisdom, strength—I lovingly impart

Take the time to listen, be still and know that I am God
Ask Me for direction—on which path to trod
I will guide you by My eye as you look to Me
You will clearly hear My voice even when you cannot see

Me:
Wind song, all night long, play a tune and sing
As the cords strum on my heart, Your praises I will bring
On wind's song, I glide along, high up in the sky
Now no longer earthbound I'll join with You to fly

May 31, 2018

John 15:5—"I am the vine; you are the branches. If you remain in me and I in you, you will bear much fruit; apart from me you can do nothing."

Ephesians 2:6-7—"And God raised us up with Christ and seated us with him in the heavenly realms in Christ Jesus, [7] in order that in the coming ages he might show the incomparable riches of his grace, expressed in his kindness to us in Christ Jesus."

Psalm 1
Isaiah 55:12
Acts 2:1-12, 4:31
Ephesians 2:4-10
John 3:5-8
1 Corinthians 2:6-16

    I was at a retreat/conference resort by myself, and they had a special building with large windows in it to reflect, pray, read, and worship. As I settled into the chair, the beauty of the lake and nature outside overwhelmed my soul with peace. It was nearing dusk outside, and the lake birds were starting to settle down. I waited to hear God's voice, but nothing came.
    People were scheduled to come in at different intervals to play an instrument and sing softly. A man came in and saw me there by myself and asked me if I minded if he played some music. I said, "That would be wonderful."
    As soon as he started to play the keyboard and softly sing, the words to this poem started to come to me. In about an hour, "Wind Song" was finished and so was his music.

The music of the night not only flowed around me, it seemed to flow through me. Worship opened the doors of heaven so I could clearly hear God's voice. It was as if the wind of the Holy Spirit was singing and I could hear the song.

Other books by Debbie Furey

About the Book—"The Rapture: Behold the Bridegroom Cometh!"
By Debbie Furey

Jesus's second coming is a "day" of darkness that will cover the earth. However, it will also be a "day" when the glory of God will rise in His people and nations will be drawn to that light. (Isaiah 60) The days leading up to the return of Christ will be a time of unprecedented harvest into the kingdom of God. Will you be ready for Christ's return?

For those who have ever wondered about the second return of Christ or questioned how to be prepared, this insightful guide uses the truths of Scripture to answer questions such as:

- What is the rapture?
- Will all Christians be taken in the rapture?
- How is Jesus' return like the "days of Noah"?
- How is the rapture a picture of the ancient Jewish wedding customs?

Author Debbie Furey has spent countless hours in prayer and study uncovering hidden prophecies throughout the Bible related to Jesus Christ's second coming. One such prophecy in the book of Ruth paints a picture of the return of the Jews coming back into their land shortly before the marriage of Jesus Christ and His church. Another prophecy is hidden in the Song of Solomon - the parable of the five wide and five foolish virgins of Matthew 25, which explains what will happen to those who are ready and those who are not.

Read about all this and more in her book: "The Rapture: Behold the Bridegroom Cometh!"

About the Book—"Refresh Me With Apples"
By Debbie Furey

A devotional in poetry of conversations with God

One thinks of prayers as talking to God, but true conversation is allowing the time to listen to the thoughts of others, as well as making our thoughts known. So, our times of prayer should be both times of speaking and listening. In putting that to practice, I have written many poems over the years that include my thoughts and what I believe to be what the Lord has shared to my heart in poetry form.

My poems answer some interesting questions:

- Can a train whistle speak to us?
- Can God speak to us?
- Did you ever hear water's song?
- What turned the tide when David battled Goliath?
- Does God cry?
- Are there rewards waiting for us in heaven?
- Was there an intruder at the Last Supper?
- Do ancient holy men of God still speak?
- What is the message of the two thieves who were crucified with Jesus?
- What will the day of the Lord be like?

Discover the answer to these questions in my book, "Refresh Me With Apples", as you seek to draw closer to the Lord.

Website: www.debbiefureysbooks.com

Milton Keynes UK
Ingram Content Group UK Ltd.
UKHW010738030424
440506UK00014B/1890